Mindfulness For Parents

Finding Your Way to a Calmer,
Happier Family

Amber Hatch

WATKINS

Sharing Wisdom Since
1893

This edition first published in the UK and USA 2017 by
Watkins, an imprint of Watkins Media Limited
19 Cecil Court
London WC2N 4EZ

enquiries@watkinspublishing.com

Design and typography copyright © Watkins Media Limited 2017

Text copyright © Amber Hatch 2017
Illustrations copyright © Alex Ogg 2017

Amber Hatch has asserted her right under the Copyright, Designs and Patents
Act 1988 to be identified as the author of this work.

Page 191: From *The Miracle of Mindfulness* by Thich Nhat Hanh, published
by Ebury. Reprinted by permission of the Random House Group Limited.
Copyright © 1975, 1976 by Thich Nhat Hanh. Preface and English translation
Copyright © 1975, 1976, 1987 by Mobi Ho. Reprinted by permission of Beacon
Press, Boston.
Pages 192–193: *The Mindful Way Through Depression: Freeing Yourself from
Chronic Unhappiness* by Williams, Teasdale, Segal and Kabat-Zinn. Reproduced
with permission of Guilford Press in the format Republish in a book via
Copyright Clearance Center.

1 3 5 7 9 10 8 6 4 2

Designed and typeset by Donald Sommerville

Printed and bound in Finland

A CIP record for this book is available from the British Library

ISBN: 978-1-78028-960-1

www.watkinspublishing.com

To Morrigan, Dougal and the little being who has grown alongside this book.

Contents

Acknowledgements

Thanks to my agent, Jane, of Graham Maw Christie, who encouraged me to get this project off the ground. Thanks to Jo Lal, Sandy Draper and everyone at Watkins Publishing – yet again it has been a pleasure to work with you!

This book has grown out of my own meditation practice, which could not have developed without the kindness and wisdom of my teachers at Samatha, who give their time so generously. I owe particular thanks to my class teacher Terry, and also to Charles King, who has taught me so much through his patience and understanding.

I am indebted to the many friends, both within Samatha and without who travel this journey alongside me, sharing their experiences and encouragement. Thanks to everyone who contributed anecdotes, thoughts and experiences for this book. Rebekah Curtis, Ben Curtis and Namaste Wiles all deserve a special mention – thank you! Also thanks to Gwil, Gareth, Jan, Bethan, Anne, Deborah, Joe and Gemma.

I've known Guin Webster from the earliest days of parenting, and our respective mindfulness journeys, and I have learnt so much from her gentle, thoughtful example. Working with Guin to establish a regular meditation group for parents was pivotal in forming this book. Thanks for her unwavering enthusiasm and support throughout! Many thanks to all the wonderful women I have met through this group; the sincerity with which they parent and practise is inspirational. I'm very grateful for the help I received from Nancy Bardacke and Maret Dymond, who generously gave up their time to share their experiences with me.

Thanks to my parents for their love and support, and especial thanks to my husband Alex. And of course none of this could be possible without my children, Morrigan and Dougal – my greatest teachers.

Introduction

When I became pregnant with my first child, I was 24 years old and extremely idealistic. I was determined to have a perfect pregnancy and empowering birth experience, and to be a great mother. I thought it would be a breeze.

I loved being pregnant. I was lucky: everything went smoothly – no morning sickness or backache, and I was riding my bike right up until week 39. I read up on active birth techniques, attended pregnancy yoga classes and became indignant at the medicalization, as I saw it, of childbirth. Birth didn't have to be painful if you did it right, the books informed me. I told my friends and family that *I* wanted to be in control when I gave birth. I decided to borrow a birth pool and have a home birth.

When labour finally kicked in, I spent the first few hours playing with the TENS machine and stamping around. But the pains were getting worse, and I was hardly dilated. This wasn't what I had expected. I hid from the midwife in another room. At last I crawled upstairs to the bathroom. The pain was so intense I was sweating all over and I thought I was about to vomit. I crouched on the landing, unable to open the bathroom door. The pain was unbearable, but even worse was my sense of failure: *I was stupid and naïve to think I would be able to handle this,* I thought. *I can't take the pain and I'm going to have to ask to be transferred to hospital.*

And then, as I doubled over with my ideals collapsing around me, a remarkable thing happened. From the depths of my despair

I had a flash of insight into what I was doing wrong: I was fighting the contractions. I was trying to tackle them head on – using my 'active birth' techniques and yoga postures *against* them. A good birth wasn't about being 'in control', after all. It was about feeling safe enough to let go. So instead of trying to move or curl up or wish myself away, at the next contraction I breathed slowly and purposefully, allowing myself to actually feel the movement surge through my abdomen. It was still challenging, yes, and scary: I didn't know what this sensation might do to me. But it was no longer excruciating. I felt the sickness pass. I made my way back downstairs and rejoined the midwife at the kitchen table. Now whenever the contractions came, I sat very still and silent and tried to welcome them.

Of course, the labour progressed and before long I was on all fours in transition. The birth pool still wasn't ready due to some water-heating glitch. At some point I had begun to vocalize. I had practised 'Oms' during pregnancy yoga. During class I had cringed, but now I appreciated the familiar way they resonated in me. And, I found that as long as I 'Ommed', and concentrated on the sound, the pain stayed at bay.

When the sound faded away, thoughts began to crowd in. I noticed that as I sank into self-pity: *Oh why is this happening to me . . . I can't cope with this . . .* then the pain surfaced abruptly. But at the times when I was able to quieten that little voice and I could simply submit to the sensation – at those moments the pain vanished. The contractions surged on and on until they rolled into one long contraction. Then, I felt so small that my sense of a separate self – that little voice – seemed to disappear entirely, and I felt an overwhelming feeling of awe at the power of the birth process. A part of me was able to observe that I had become a mere vehicle for the mechanisms of the universe, which were grinding away, like cogs, inside me.

At last, the pool was filled, and eventually, my baby girl was born in the water, weighing 9lb 13oz.

THE JOURNEY BEGINS

Why have I told you my birth story? Of course, this event marked the beginning of parenthood. But it also marked another watershed moment, although I was unable to explain it in those terms: it was the moment that I first became aware of the tremendous power of mindfulness. With very little experience or understanding of meditation, I knew that through letting go of that intellectualizing self, I had come into contact with something very special. Whatever it was, while I was in touch with it, it was powerful enough to wipe away the agony of birth pains.

My birth experience *was* empowering, but not in the way I had imagined. I had expected to feel that *I* had achieved this success through good planning, confidence and determination. But in hindsight, it was *surrendering* to the process that enabled me to have the kind of birth I wanted. It wasn't *me* that had birthed my baby – not the 'me' that read books and wrote birth plans, anyway. It was something much bigger than 'me' – and 'my' role in the process was simply to not stand in its way. So, although the experience was empowering in a way, it was also incredibly humbling. And I am so grateful for that lesson at the start of my journey into parenthood. In the months and years that followed I came to learn that staying in control and high ideals aren't what make a good parent, any more than they make a good birth. A birth experience can be embraced, whether it's at home or in hospital, low-intervention or highly medicalized. It's the ability to welcome whatever is happening in the present moment that makes us truly able to rise to the challenges of parenthood.

So, for me, mindfulness and parenting have been bound together right from the very beginning; and, while I have never had the message brought home to me quite so emphatically as it was during my first labour, I have continually found that when I stop fighting reality and start accepting it, then everything goes a whole lot more smoothly. And mindfulness – especially when we set out to practise it – is a way of helping us to do just that.

I believe that we can all benefit from this simple, yet utterly transformative skill. I hope that by sharing my experiences and those of other parents, we can explore how mindfulness can be applied to all areas of family life, for the benefit of ourselves, our children and the wider world. Mindfulness, and especially mindful parenting, has been a precious gift to me, and I hope to share this gift with as many people as possible.

Who Is This Book For?

This book is for people who are interested in practising mindfulness while raising children. As the title suggests, this book is primarily for parents (or parents-to-be), though other people who look after children, for example grandparents or professional childcare givers, may also find it useful.

Although I've talked about my own birthing experience, this book does not, in fact, cover the use of mindfulness in pregnancy and childbirth in any great detail. I believe that mindfulness is an exceptional resource to use in labour for all types of birth experience. However, this subject merits a book of its own, and indeed there are some excellent books that discuss how mindfulness can be used in preparation for birth (see the resources section on pages 244–245).

Mindfulness can be used as a guiding principle for parenting throughout family life, whatever the age of your children. In the main, this book draws examples from the first few years of parenthood, as this intense period of parenting is a time when parents often need to find new ways to deal with the challenges they face.

This book is a resource for all parents, whether you are

- New to both parenthood and mindfulness.
- Already a parent, but new to mindfulness.
- Already practising mindfulness, but are looking for help incorporating this into your new family life.

How to Use This Book

The first chapter is an introduction to mindfulness and mindful parenting, and sets these within the context of Buddhism and the modern world. Chapter 2 explains how we can incorporate mindfulness into our daily life. Chapters 3–9 provide an in-depth look at the different opportunities and challenges facing mindful parents. Chapter 10 considers how a commitment to ethical living can support mindfulness, and Chapter 11 discusses introducing mindfulness to children. The final four chapters, 12–15, consider ways to deepen your meditation practice, through establishing formal meditation, seeking teaching support and going on retreat, all in the context of practising within the family.

Readers who are just starting out on their parenting journey and are new to the concept of mindfulness, will find the entire book relevant to them. Readers with slightly older babies and/ or children may like to skip over Chapter 3, which focuses on the postnatal period. Those who have already established their own meditation practice may not need the meditation described in Chapter 12, but will probably find the practical advice in Chapter 13 helpful, as it considers how to establish meditation alongside the demands of the family.

The chapters are arranged to be read from start to finish. I'd also suggest dipping in to chapters that catch your eye at that moment; perhaps the subject of managing difficult behaviour or going on retreat is of especial interest to you right now, in which case it is fine to pick and mix.

Sometimes I refer to your baby or child as 'he' or 'she' (rather than 'they'). I've roughly alternated this by chapter, to try to keep it fair! I also sometimes refer to 'your child' or 'your children'. But the examples I give apply to both boys and girls, and however many children you have.

PARENTS' VOICES

Throughout this book you will find anecdotes, tips and insights from other parents who are exploring the benefits and challenges of mindfulness within the family. Some of these parents have started their meditative journey since I've known them; others I have met through meditation. Some of them are highly experienced meditation teachers, while others are at the beginning of their mindfulness journey. I have got to know many parents through Samatha Meditation, and especially while helping to organize the annual family retreat at the Samatha retreat centre in Wales. Helping to establish a family meditation group in Oxford, where parents can practise alongside their children, has been a valuable learning experience, and I am very grateful to the parents who have shared their experience of this project with me. I wouldn't have been able to write this book without the help of all these parents, some of whom have spent many hours with me discussing aspects of parenting and practice. I am very grateful that they have shared their stories with me, and I hope you will find their words as inspiring as I do.

I

What Is Mindful Parenting?

The task of raising children is not easy, and the stakes are high: the way we interact with our children in the early years is critical to our relationship with them as they get older and also for their development.

Parents often need to learn new techniques and hone skills to rise to the challenges of family life, and this is especially true in the first few years. Babies and young children are very needy and demand a huge amount of our attention and resources, which makes this period very intense.

HOW CAN MINDFULNESS HELP US PARENT?

Among other things, mindfulness can help us to

- stay calm in a crisis
- feel more connected to our children and other people
- be patient
- throw ourselves into an activity
- not say something we may regret
- keep a sense of perspective

These are qualities that can improve life for anybody – but parents will especially recognize the significance of these benefits. Being around children is like living with the volume turned up. Everything is more extreme and children can court the full range of human emotions each and every day. Of course everyone –

whether a parent or not – experiences challenge at times. But when you become a parent it can be surprising (and sometimes overwhelming) to find out just how often you will have to deal with tricky situations. Parents may be vomited on, screamed at, poked in the eye, woken up several times in the night; they will have to tear apart children who are trying to bite each other; they will hear 'I want that lolly' 27 times; they will be humiliated in the supermarket; they will hear 'I hate you' and 'I love you' in the same minute; they will have to catch a child who's falling off a wall; they will, at times, need to do everything one-handed; they will need to read the same story six times in a row; they will have to rescue a child who is gagging; comfort one who is crying, soothe one who is terrified of the dark; they will have to navigate through perpetual noise and chaos and mess – all this and more – perhaps in the course of a single day. Mindfulness can help parents to cope with all of that.

I was having a hard time with feeling very irritated with my children . . . and I felt I needed a way to create more space between my feelings of irritation and my angry reaction – and to respond to my children more thoughtfully. I began to see that mindfulness could help me do that.
Guin, MBCP meditation teacher and mum of three

Mindfulness can give us a little bit of distance – that sense of perspective I mentioned earlier (see page 9). But I don't mean being *disengaged* from our children, far from it. Instead it helps us to maintain a calm place inside ourselves, from where we can *be* with our children, but not caught up in their drama. It can stop us getting caught up in our own drama, too.

This is not a new idea – parents everywhere already intuitively know that keeping our wits about us helps us manage. What *is* new, perhaps, is the idea that we can *actively increase our ability* to keep our wits about us. We can have more presence of mind, simply by trying to have more presence of mind. (I talk more about the cultivation of mindfulness overleaf.) And when we unite this practice with the job of parenting, we end up with a very powerful tool indeed.

All parents use and experience mindfulness – even if they have never heard of the word. This book will help you to recognize that quality when it arises so that you can begin to see how powerful it really is. It will also help you to cultivate it so that you can raise mindfulness more often, and maintain it for longer, even when the pasta is boiling over and the baby is crying.

For me mindfulness as a parent is about being clear that I'm taking on a role, which is not fixed but instead requires me to respond to the moment.
Gwil, meditation teacher and dad to a son, 6, and daughter, 3

SO WHAT IS MINDFULNESS?

In ordinary English parlance, 'being mindful' means remembering or thinking about something, and often, allowing that remembrance to influence your actions. For example: 'Please be mindful of the neighbours when you play your drums.'

The 'mindfulness' that concerns us is a bit subtler. It is a translation from the Pali word *sati*. Pali is the language of Buddhism and sati is a technical description of a mind state from Buddhist psychology (see pages 13–15 for more about the Buddhist context of mindfulness). As is often the case with translation, there is not an exact English word that holds the full range of meaning, but the scholar T. W. Rhys Davids established 'mindfulness', as the translation of sati around 100 years ago, and academics and Buddhist practitioners have been using it ever since.[1] The definition of sati is somewhat difficult to pin down, but it describes a more encompassing state than our common use of the word mindful.

Sati, or mindfulness, as I shall now call it, describes the quality of mind when we have an awareness of what is happening in the present moment. This can include an awareness of our body, our thoughts and our environment. It's not a fixed, concentrated attention. Instead it has a much lighter touch: it's an expansive observance of the goings-on of the moment. Like the original English use of the word, mindfulness does have something of the quality of remembrance or recollection, but we do not restrict it to specifics: we are 'remembering' our capacity to be aware.

WHAT HAPPENS WHEN WE ARE MINDFUL?

When we are mindful, we experience life as it is actually happening. As mindfulness deepens, our sense of a separate self diminishes, allowing us to feel more connected to the world around us. This sense of being fully present in the moment makes everything feel more intense, more real. When we are mindful we can watch where our thoughts are going, rather than be swept along with them. We are also more aware of our feelings, whether they are joy, sadness, contentedness or anger. And when we are being mindful, it is easier to choose whether or not to act on those feelings.

Meditation allows me to ground myself, and feel more able to cope with daily life. Sometimes moments of clarity arise and it's possible to see what needs to be done in a particular situation.
Jan, mum to Josia, 8, and Hannah, 5

CULTIVATING MINDFULNESS

Mindfulness is not just a pleasant state that sometimes graces us; we can actually *cultivate* it. Although mindfulness can potentially exist whatever we are thinking of or doing, the best way to help it arise is to bring our attention back to the present moment. Becoming aware of our breath is probably the simplest way to do this. The breath is always with us, yet every single one is unique. This makes it an ideal choice for helping us regain awareness. Unlike other qualities such as patience or generosity (which we sometimes have to work a bit harder for), mindfulness is unique: as soon as we notice our mind has wandered, mindfulness has returned. Inevitably, though, we soon forget what we are doing and our thoughts wander off in another direction, often to the past or the future or some other imagined scenario. Bringing our attention back to our breath helps mindfulness arise again, and mental distractions pass through us. When we set out to bring our attention to the present moment over and over again, we can describe this activity as 'practising mindfulness'. Soon the process becomes a mental habit, and mindfulness arises more easily and more often.

Despite our best intentions, it is often difficult to remember to be mindful, so we can help things along by setting aside specific times to practise. One of the best ways to do this is by sitting quietly for a few minutes each day, simply with the intention of keeping the attention on the breath, for example. This type of sitting practice is what is meant by the term meditation. Actually, we can meditate at any time of the day, for as long or short as we want, in whatever the conditions happen to be. But sitting in silence in formal meditation, without other distractions, helps us stay focused and committed to the practice. I'll talk more about sitting meditation in Chapter 12.

ROOTS IN BUDDHISM

Mindfulness has become very popular in recent years and is sometimes portrayed as a 'brand new' innovation in mental health and wellbeing. In fact, mindfulness is not new at all. It has been taught and practised as part of a Buddhist system of psychology for over two-and-a-half millennia. Buddhist texts provide an extensive explanation of the way in which mindfulness (and other positive qualities of the mind) can be cultivated in order to reduce mental suffering and increase happiness.

Modern pioneers, in particular Jon Kabat-Zinn in the US and Mark Williams in the UK, discovered mindfulness when looking for alternative ways to treat stress and depression.[2] They saw how practising mindfulness provided patients with new mental skills that could help them break cycles of negative thinking. They also found that mindfulness could increase happiness levels in people without mental health problems.[3] They developed a system for practising mindfulness based on what they considered the most effective elements of Buddhist teaching, leaving behind many of the accompanying practices and guidelines, and certainly all of the cultural trappings and belief systems.

In particular, the well-known MBSR and MBCT programmes developed by Kabat-Zinn and Williams do not include any instructions for ethical living. In Buddhism, ethical living is seen as an important aspect of the path to reduce personal suffering, and it is considered to work in conjunction with mindfulness, as an aid to that practice. Kabat-Zinn, Williams and others have made mindfulness significantly more accessible in the West, and perhaps this success has only been possible through its 'secularization'.

However, I believe that it is limiting to shut our minds to potential sources of wisdom. In the case of mindfulness, I think it is unhelpful to side with any one camp – whether that is Buddhist or non-Buddhist. So later in this book I will return to Buddhist ideas and consider how we can influence our mindfulness practice through developing accompanying positive mind states (see Chapter 4) and through different ways of living (see Chapter 10). That doesn't mean you have to be Buddhist to benefit from mindful parenting – I don't take any teaching as doctrine, and I won't be asking you to sign up to any kind of belief. But all parents can benefit from the increased self-awareness that mindfulness helps raise, regardless of their religious point of view.

I think a lot of daily life with a baby can feel challenging, and I am inclined to feel it is always like that. However, mindfulness opens my eyes to reality and in it I see the many wonderful aspects of my baby and of being a mummy that I think I might otherwise miss.
Emily, mum to Owen, 2

PARENTING AS A MEDITATION PRACTICE

At first glance it may seem as if family life is not the best place to try to pursue a mindfulness practice. The chaos and noise may seem completely at odds with our idea of a serene figure sitting quietly in a lotus position. You may think that this book will be about making the best of a bad job – how to adapt a meditation practice in whatever way we can so that we can at least get some benefit.

Undoubtedly there are many challenges when pursuing a practice as a parent, but there are also unique and profound opportunities too. In their book *Everyday Blessings*, Jon and Myra Kabat-Zinn refer to parenting as an '18-year retreat.'[4] I think this reflects the fact that when we bring mindfulness to parenting, we are essentially choosing to use this task as a meditation practice in itself. Considering what an all-encompassing job it is to raise children, a commitment to doing it with mindfulness means embarking on a path of major inner work.

Jon Kabat-Zinn likens the job of parenting to a sailor making use of the wind. Even though the wind may blow in all sorts of different directions, and at different speeds, the skilled sailor may still use it to reach a certain point on the shore.[5] I like this image a lot. The wind itself doesn't have an agenda. It doesn't care about you getting to your destination. And, to a large extent, your children are oblivious to your journey too. They will throw all sorts of challenges into your path, some of which seem to knock you off balance. But with mindfulness, we can keep in mind the long-term goals of our parenting, and also our own long-term goals: whichever way it blows, we can still harness the wind to take us in the direction that we want to go.

Every time our children rub up against us or disturb our calm in some way, we will produce a reaction. And if we learn to be curious about that reaction, hold it and examine it mindfully, rather than just acting it out, then we begin to understand ourselves better. The more often we can keep calm and connected in a crisis, the better for both us *and* our children – because it is the accumulation of all these little incidents that defines our relationship with our children and helps to build their characters. But if we do lose it from time to time, then we'll get the opportunity to try again the next time – children are very resilient!

The other wonderful thing about children is that they are extremely responsive. They really do want us to be great parents, and they'll reward our efforts to be mindful with their love and delight and trust, almost instantly.

SUMMARY

- *Mindfulness helps us to parent by keeping us calm and encouraging a sense of perspective.*
- *Mindfulness is the state of mind when our attention is on our present moment experience, and we are aware of ourselves.*
- *We can cultivate mindfulness by practising it, and encourage it to arise more often and more easily.*
- *Mindfulness allows us to experience everything more fully and feel more connected to the people and the world around us.*
- *Mindfulness originates from Buddhism, but you don't have to be a Buddhist to benefit from it.*
- *Committing to parent mindfully means embarking on a journey with vast potential for growth.*

2

How to Practise Mindfulness – Moment by Moment

Some people think that you need a lot of spare time to meditate. Actually, you don't need any spare time at all. This is because you can practise mindfulness at any time throughout the day, just as you go about your normal business. In fact, as you get more used to it, you can aim to practise mindfulness all the time.

USING TIME MORE EFFECTIVELY

You may even find that practising mindfulness *frees up* time – because your increased awareness and concentration help you to use your time more effectively. For example, I used to be extremely disorganized and scatty, and each day I would spend a significant amount of time looking for things I had lost: my phone, my keys, a screwdriver. Mindfulness has not yet made me a tidy person, but I can see that I spend much less time looking for things. That's because I am more mindful about where and how I put them down.

This rather practical benefit of mindfulness is by no means the only way that practice can help us use time more effectively. Mindfulness can help us sleep better, feel more energized, spend less time worrying about things ... the list goes on. Practising mindfulness will also help us develop our concentration so that we are able to focus better.

PRACTICE AND PARENTING

Children will love you being more mindful. *Your* moment-to-moment mindfulness is exactly what *they* want, right now. Your children will sense your increased awareness and respond to it, in every moment that you are present with them. It brings instant results. Though for the vast majority of the time they will be oblivious to the fact that you are making any special effort to maintain awareness.

Children can act as our teachers in the sense that they show us how to be present. During play, children live fully in the moment – throwing themselves into their activity without any of the self-consciousness that we adults find so hard to abandon. When they invite us to play with them, we can learn a lot from their example. And they continually call us back into the present with their constant clamouring for our attention.

I am brought back to mindfulness when I have something
on my mind and my son wants to play with me. When
he asks what things are, things I usually take for granted,
I remember to be interested in even the little things in life.
Kate, mum to Zach, 2½

Chapters 3–9 will look in detail at how we can make use of mindfulness in particular areas of parenting. But for now I want to look at some general points about maintaining mindfulness during the day.

HOW DO WE PRACTISE MINDFULNESS IN OUR DAY?

The instruction is quite simple: whenever we can, we need to bring our attention back to the task at hand. The wonderful thing about mindfulness is that as soon as we notice that we are not being mindful, then that, in itself, is a moment of mindfulness. However, it can just as easily slip away again, especially as you first start to practise. So we need to keep on bringing our attention back to the present moment and the task at hand, again and again and again. Many people find that the breath is an excellent focal point. It's always there, and it's always unique. 'The present moment' can sometimes seem a little too abstract as a concept, but the breath is very simple to find.

ONE THING AT A TIME

Many meditation teachers will tell you that the key to maintaining mindfulness is to do one thing at a time. The idea is that it is much easier to keep our attention on an activity if we are only doing one. So, when we are eating, we just eat, focusing our attention on the temperature of the food, the texture in our mouths, the taste . . . and so on. When we are washing dishes, we just do that, concentrating on the way the sponge wipes away the crumbs, the way the foam slides off the plate, etc.

As a parent, I find this instruction slightly absurd. Parenting is virtually synonymous with multitasking. When I'm eating, I'm also checking to make sure that my children aren't choking or flicking peas at each other. When I'm washing the dishes, I'm also looking through the window to watch my children jump on the trampoline. When we are with our children, and they are clamouring for our attention and help, we have our own list of jobs that we want to get done. If we have more than one child, then we are regularly torn in two or more different directions. So – does this mean that we can't practise mindfulness? Of course not! It just makes it harder, but whenever mindfulness is harder, that's when it's more useful.

And anyway the idea that *anyone* can simply do one thing at a time is rather simplistic, whether or not they are a parent. When we are eating, we are doing lots of things: we are breathing and sitting and tasting and listening and sensing and smelling and tensing some muscles and relaxing others . . . there are lots of things going on, even if we aren't intervening in a food fight. But it is useful to try to keep our attention on one thing at a time, at the same time as having a broad awareness of the other things around us.

TIP: To-do list

I find it really helpful to have a to-do list on the wall. I have a small whiteboard and marker. I make sections for different areas of my life and I put on tasks that will be achievable over the next day or two. It's tempting to put up 'redecorate the kids' room' or some other aspiration – but this isn't helpful. Keep it realistic. Once I've written down the tasks, I find I can let go of them more easily, and I don't have to keep reminding myself what's coming up next. This helps me keep my awareness on the task at hand. By the way, I also like to put up easy routine tasks such as *meditate, wash dishes, make packed lunch*, because it makes me feel productive when I wipe them off! It's also a great idea to include less obvious tasks like 'read my son a story' or 'quality playtime with daughter'. These 'jobs' are just as, if not more, important than phoning the dentist, but they so easily get swept aside by the business of the day.

And there *are* things that we can do to make it easier to limit simultaneous tasks. Perhaps the most important thing is simply to bear in mind the value of doing just one thing at a time. Buddhist psychology teaches that the mind is in fact only capable of holding one object of attention at any one time. This means that although it feels as if we are thinking about two (or more) different things at once, in actual fact we are flicking between them at a terrific speed. This is really tiring. It also means that we are doing each individual job less efficiently, as we are not giving it our sustained attention. The total time taken for the jobs may even end up being longer.

Remembering that it's better to do just one job at a time can encourage us to find more opportunities to slow down.

---

*Sometimes I find myself getting into a frenzy of activity,
and when the workload finally starts to drop off, I look for
more jobs that I think I 'need' to do.*
Kirsten, mum to Eva, 5, and Josh, 3

It's important to notice when the jobs are diminishing, and instead of searching out more, learn to be grateful and appreciate the one we are doing.

YOU ARE ALLOWED TO THINK

When I first found out about mindfulness, I got very confused about whether it was acceptable to think about anything at all. The instruction is to bring the mind back into the present moment as often as we can, and not get carried away on past memories or planning for the future, or any other imagined scenario.

But you are allowed to think sometimes! Our brain is an amazing tool, and we often need it to work things out for us. Sometimes it is appropriate to go over past events or plan for the future. We need to use our brain to conceptualize abstract ideas and to play around with them. However, we need to be careful that our brain is not getting the better of us. Thoughts can often entice us away from the experience of real life, as it is happening. There are times when it is absolutely appropriate for you to be figuring out how to pay the gas bill, but that time is not when you are getting ready for your son's swimming class. Being mindful when thinking can help keep us on track, but this can be particularly tricky as thoughts can be intoxicating and make us forget to be aware.

I think it becomes a way of being over time if you persistently turn your mind to the present moment. Eventually the mind stays there more naturally and it is no longer an effort.

Deborah, meditation teacher and mum to Jesse, 20, and Rowan, 17

TIP: Attaching mindfulness to an activity

A good way to practise mindfulness is to 'attach' a mindfulness practice to an individual activity. Ideally, we would be trying to be mindful all the time. But sometimes it's worth earmarking a certain activity for special mindful attention. It doesn't matter what you choose – it could be hanging out the washing or walking up the stairs or reading to your child. You may find it helpful to keep this as a regular mindfulness activity, so that you practise every single time you do it.

This kind of practice is a sort of halfway house between formal meditation and moment-to-moment mindfulness. You get many of the benefits of formal sitting (though perhaps not with the same depth of relaxation and concentration), yet you can do it while carrying on with your day-to-day business.

One Thursday I was feeling stressed and caught myself rushing about too much. So I decided to slow the day down – walking upstairs, not dashing, and doing household tasks mindfully – and make Thursdays 'slow Thursdays'. I also try to be slow and mindful on other days, but Thursdays have become a focal point. When

I master Thursdays as slow days I will add another day,
and then another, until my whole week is more mindful!
Kate, mum to Zach, 2½

'BELLS OF MINDFULNESS'

One of my favourite teachings is from the mindfulness teacher
Thich Nhat Hanh. In his book *Peace is Every Step* he explains
how in the East, bells are regularly used as an aid to mindfulness.[6]
Hearing the bell's sound brings our attention back to the present.
As we don't hear bells that often in the West, Thich Nhat Hanh
suggests that we can use other events as 'bells of mindfulness'. The
red traffic light is a perfect example. Whenever we see it, we can
let it serve as a reminder for us to be mindful. We can choose
whatever we like, though something that crops up regularly is
best.

Not long after I had read this I came to realize that I had found
my own bell of mindfulness: it was my daughter's scream. At
the time she was a very passionate toddler, who was regularly
frustrated by things not going her way. Every time she screamed
I was reminded to breathe and to raise awareness. It turned out to
be an extremely helpful bell, as during her tantrums was the exact
moment that I needed the most mindfulness of all.

When you see your child as a 'bell of mindfulness' you
find that the 'bell' is ringing all day long encouraging
you to wake up!
Ben, dad to Leo, 6

SUMMARY

- *During the day you can encourage mindfulness at anytime by bringing yourself back to the present moment. The breath is a great place to focus your attention.*
- *'Attach' mindfulness to certain activities, such as vacuuming or hanging out the washing. Try to make a special effort every time you do this activity.*
- *Find a 'bell of mindfulness' that occurs regularly, which will remind you to be mindful.*

3

Mindfulness in the Early Weeks

You hold your new baby in your arms, and you gaze into her face. You look at the way her lips purse and relax, her eyes flutter under their lids, her translucent skin, the soft curve of her ear, her tiny eyelashes. What new parent does not spend time doing this? We examine every tiny detail, wanting to learn this new face, to inscribe it on our mind. For most parents, it is very natural for a high degree of mindfulness to occur at this time. We are utterly absorbed by our baby's face, and yet at the same time we notice every little change. We feel the soft warmth of the bundle in our arms; we hear her breathing. We notice our own feelings too – perhaps joy and contentment. We are utterly present in this moment.

New babies can teach us an awful lot about mindfulness. Most parents, even those who have never heard of mindfulness, intuitively understand that something special happens when we take the time to get to know our babies. And this 'getting to know' – this *learning* that we are compelled to do – is only possible if we really look to see what is happening right now. How does she wrinkle her forehead? How does she push out her lips? What is that little sound she makes, as she shifts her torso? If we don't actually take note of the reality, then all we are doing is creating a construct based on some other ideas about who our baby is. In fact, the same is true of all learning. All learning is based on a foundation of mindfulness. We need to bring our awareness to the reality of the moment, and to notice without judgement or preconceptions.

In other circumstances, it is all too easy for us not to bother to look too closely. We prefer to rely on old assumptions about how the world works, which makes it harder for us to learn anything new, or to understand things more clearly. With a baby, however, we intuitively know that this is too important a task. We are not prepared to rely on old assumptions – we are naturally motivated to get to know exactly who our baby is, right now. And for that we raise a huge amount of mindfulness.

GETTING TO KNOW YOUR BABY EVERY DAY

This unique experience gives us a massive head start with establishing a mindfulness practice. Even if you are already used to practising, I still think it's relevant to talk about establishing something new, as everything will need to change and shift as you learn how to fit this new baby into your life.

You will often hear people jokingly moan about babies: 'When you think you understand them, they go ahead and change again!' It's true. Babies are changing all the time – especially in the first few weeks. And sometimes we can feel as if this constant change is undermining our attempts to be competent parents. We may feel disheartened when a strategy for soothing – which worked fine last week – now has no influence. But this constant change is actually a massive aid to us in maintaining mindfulness: it forces us to keep on looking and keep on learning.

BEING WITH BABY

Babies force us to slow right down – virtually to a halt. For first-time parents this can come as a major surprise. I had some grand ideas about all the jobs and activities I would do while on maternity leave. I simply did not anticipate the sheer amount of time that I would have to spend feeding my baby. Literally hours on end! There was no time for me to shower or put the kettle on, let alone write a novel and learn Spanish, as I had planned!

And it's not just mothers who experience this slowing down. Fathers will also find that every task takes 10 times as long to perform, and the most mundane ones, such as preparing food and doing the laundry, become significant achievements. This sudden change of pace has a big impact on our levels of mindfulness.

We'll probably notice that our mind is going faster than our activity. I'm reminded of my sister who had to relocate to Mexico soon after she had her first son. She told me that whenever she sat down to breastfeed him, she would look around the room and notice all the jobs that needed doing. 'Ah yes, that needs packing, and that and that . . .' and then she'd just have to resign herself to the fact that nothing could happen for the next 30 to 40 minutes.

Everything happens more slowly so you have time to pay attention to each task. You are not being overloaded with stimuli, and eventually that may mean that your mind becomes less frenzied, as it has to deal with fewer issues and less excitement. You may welcome this change and enjoy the slower pace, or it may be that the practicality of caring for a baby feels stifling.

SOCIETY MAKES MOTHERHOOD HARD

Western society is extraordinary in its lack of support for new mums. Many dads go back to work after a couple of weeks of paternity leave, but the new mum is no longer allowed to return to her workplace, as long as she has baby with her. Socializing with colleagues is difficult, and much of her previous social activity is now no longer feasible. It is likely that she barely knows her neighbours and it may be that her family live many miles away. After the initial flurry of visits to welcome the new baby, motherhood can begin to feel lonely. And this is at a time when mums are in such great need of practical help and moral support. No wonder so many mums find parenthood isolating and dispiriting.

BEING ON CALL 24/7

When you are caring for a baby – nothing can be taken for granted. Your baby needs to be helped to sleep, to feed, to move and be kept clean. She needs to be provided with just the right amount of stimulation. She may need holding for much of the day (and night). You have to monitor her needs *all the time*. Even when you are not actively on duty, you are still on call. Another way of putting this is that you have some awareness – or mindfulness – of your baby at every moment of the day, even when you are asleep! This means that parents of new babies are very well placed to develop high levels of mindfulness. We are continually being brought back into the present moment.

However, this ongoing requirement to be mindful of another being can be extraordinarily tiring. Your baby doesn't know or care if it is 4 p.m. or 4 a.m. She needs you to attend to her as and when. There is no let-up: a baby can't survive for long without you watching over her. In physical terms, the disrupted sleep can leave you very depleted, and this, along with the psychological strain of such responsibility, can take its toll.

FOCUSED ATTENTION AND BROADER AWARENESS

I think that babies can help us to be more mindful, which ultimately leads to more happiness. However, it would be rash of me to imply that this will happen quickly and easily. The fact is that when we suddenly drop all our old occupations (work, hobbies and social life), we may not realize that we are also letting go of our strategies for dealing with the world. We are suddenly faced with the experience, not just of being with our new baby, but also of being with ourselves. And that can be unsettling. You may resist the change, and feel bored or lonely or insecure. And if you start feeling trapped, it can be very scary indeed. Virtually all the mums I know have felt like this at times. I certainly have. It's a very common scenario, particularly for first-time mothers.

I think it helps to understand that these troubling feelings arise because you are no longer occupying yourself with the distractions of your previous life. That way you can make use of your growing mindfulness to watch them arise – without judgement. In the same way that you are curious about what makes your baby tick, try to be curious about yourself and your feelings – even the unpleasant ones.

But also it's important to remember that just because you now have a baby, you don't have to give up all the things you used to find interesting. I am not for one minute suggesting that you have to place all your attention on your baby all the time (if you don't want to). That's not what being mindful is about.

There are times when you need to give your baby your full attention, such as when you are latching her on to the breast or changing her nappy. And there are other times when you are perfectly at liberty to place your attention elsewhere. But while you are focusing your attention on something else – chatting to a friend, perhaps, or gardening, or going shopping – you can also keep a broad awareness of where your baby is and what she is doing and needing right now.

TIP: Keeping baby close

Carrying your baby in a sling either on your front or back allows you to concentrate on the task at hand – perhaps a household chore, or pushing an older child on the swing – and maintain that deep connection with your baby. When I carried my younger son in a sling while giving attention to my daughter, I was aware of his warmth on my back and the feel of his body relaxed against mine. If he began to fidget, my broad awareness of him meant that I could shift my focus back toward him and attend to his needs.

MAKING TIME FOR PRACTICE

If you are used to practising formal meditation regularly, or perhaps spending time each day doing yoga, then the first few weeks after your baby's arrival will almost certainly throw all of that into confusion. It is amazing that such small beings can create such chaos. You will probably find that timings are very unpredictable, and if you have a chance for some time to yourself while your baby is sleeping, then you will probably want to sleep yourself! In Chapter 13 I discuss in detail how we might carve out time for formal practice amid family life. But in these early weeks, you will probably have to accept the fact that it will be difficult to hold down a regular practice. So, instead, in the early weeks earmark routines such as nappy changes or feeding your baby as opportunities to be especially mindful.

FEEDING WITH MINDFULNESS

Feeding your baby can be a natural time for mindfulness. Because it happens regularly throughout the day, you will have lots of opportunities to hone your skills. When my first child was born, I felt I had to prove myself by being very active. One morning, when she was six weeks old I happened to be heading off to London to visit a friend. She was in a sling on my front, as I walked down the road. Then she woke up and started crying. *Oh no*. I thought, *If I turn back now to feed her that will set me back an hour or so*. So I made some adjustments to my clothing and my sling and I managed to latch her on where I stood. Now she could suck away to her heart's content, and I could get on with walking to the coach stop. Once I had discovered how to do this, I breastfed her in the sling a lot. In fact, when I knew she wanted a feed I'd often put her in the sling, so I could stay on my feet and carry on with chores around the house.

With my son, however, I had no inclination to do this whatsoever. Having the chance to sit on the sofa and feed him was

MEDITATION PRACTICE:
A meditation on feeding your baby

Choose a place to sit that will allow you to be comfortable. Pay attention to how your seat supports you. Now consider how your arms or any cushions support your baby. Can she move her head to and from the nipple or teat? As you hold your baby, feel her body against yours. Can you feel her warmth? Wherever your fingers touch, feel the fabric of her clothing, or skin or hair. What is the texture?

Watch her as she sucks for milk. Does she drink quickly or slowly? Consider how this milk that nurtures her has come to be. How it connects her to the wider world of plants and animals and the heat of the sun.

Bring your attention to your baby's breath, and to your own breath.

Notice how your baby is satisfied as she drinks. How does her body change with the intake of liquid and air? Is she tense or relaxed?

Notice the sensations in your own body. Do they mirror your baby's? Or are they different? If there is stiffness or discomfort anywhere in your body, spend a moment noticing it.

Notice the quality of your breath. Notice the quality of your baby's breath.

a glorious oasis of calm in the day. Setting this as a standard for feeds sent a very strong signal to everybody, including me, that feeding time was time for quiet. My daughter, who was by now aged three, learnt that Mummy would not be getting up from the sofa until her brother was finished.

Feeding (by either bottle or breast) is a great opportunity to have a mindful connection with your baby. You will undoubtedly find your own way of making this time special. When we simply decide to feed our baby without doing anything else, then it is not difficult to raise mindfulness. This is especially true if your baby is wide-eyed and gazing up at you! Mindfulness may also be helpful if feeding times are difficult for some reason. Try to let go of any expectations about how the feed will go, and simply notice and respond to what is happening in the here and now. The meditation on the previous page is not meant to be followed rigidly; it simply provides some ideas that you might find useful while feeding your baby. Or you may simply like to keep in touch with your breath whenever you remember.

When I was pregnant with my youngest I imagined I was going to use times when I was breastfeeding as a space for formal practice, but actually that turned out to be the worst time, as feeding my baby was very stressful ... It would have helped me to have a few different ideas about times that might work for formal practice rather than anticipating one time that then didn't work.

Guin, MBCP meditation teacher and mum of three

ESTABLISHING A ROUTINE

Perhaps one of the most shocking things about new babies is their complete unpredictability. They seemingly have no idea whether it is night or day, and they can go from gurgling and contented to screaming with hunger in the blink of an eye.

Being continually caught on the hop can be very tiring. Even if you don't think you are a very routine-y type person, you almost certainly do have habits and patterns that you take for granted. For example, most people eat a certain number of meals per day at roughly the same times. You probably go to sleep at around the same time, in the same place each day. Perhaps you have a shower and brush your teeth as soon as you get up. At least, this is how you used to live. Now you have a baby in the house, everything goes topsy-turvy. You may find yourself falling asleep on the sofa at 11 a.m., be lucky to get to shower at all, let alone first thing, and 'a meal' means whatever can be torn open and stuffed in your mouth while running to pick up a screaming baby.

As a general rule, we humans love routine. On a practical level, routine helps us to allocate time for the activities we need and want to do throughout the day. On a mental level, it takes the stress out of making decisions for every single little thing. ('What time should I have my breakfast? What should I have for my breakfast? Which plate should I use? Where should I eat?') Organizing these types of tasks from scratch takes an awful lot of mental energy. Routines also make us feel secure and comfortable. And from that base of familiarity, we can enjoy small divergences from the routine – such as a lie-in or a take-out or a visit to relatives.

Routines allow us to rely on existing decisions and assumptions, and so save our energy for more important tasks. When people go on a meditation retreat, they find that the day is very well structured, with meals and meetings arranged for precise times. This consistent framework takes the worry out of providing for our basic needs, and frees up space for being mindful, as we don't have to spend time thinking about where our next meal is coming from. I think it's important to talk about routines in a book about mindfulness, as this kind of predictability really does help us. Routines can make it more likely for us to fit in a regular formal practice, and they also make it easier to be mindful in a moment-to-moment way. For this reason, we need to recognize that a new baby in the house can make it very difficult to maintain a practice. It can be very hard to raise mindfulness when we suddenly realize we are about to faint from hunger because we haven't eaten for eight hours. Don't worry! Things will settle down once family life returns to, or arrives at, a new rhythm. And there are things you can do to gently help it along. The first thing is to recognize the value of routines in the first place!

When I had my first baby, I wanted to be very responsive to her needs. I wanted her to sleep when she was tired, eat when she was hungry, and so on. So I thought that trying to impose some kind of routine was in conflict with a truly baby-led approach. Before long, I saw how misguided I was. What I ended up with was a baby who was screaming throughout much of the day and evening because she was so wound up that she couldn't go to sleep at all. And the fact that I wasn't giving her a dark quiet space in the evening was making things worse.

When she was about four months old I realized that while I thought I was emulating some kind of 'natural' way of parenting, actually I wasn't. I considered how it must have been for our pre-civilization ancestral babies – being raised in what would become central Africa – and I realized that those babies would have been brought up in very consistent routines. For a start, at the equator, the sun would have gone down every night around 6 p.m. and up every morning 12 hours later. And it would have been *dark*. OK, so there might have been a fire and some activity around that, but the business of the day would be over. And during the daytime, activities and faces and the environment would be consistent and familiar. This is the kind of world that babies have evolved to expect when they pop out.

It is common for the world to revolve around a single baby. Although in the early weeks it's likely dad may start to have some time constraints imposed by work, it's quite possible to let your baby dictate when everything happens. New mums are told, 'sleep when baby sleeps'. When I had my second child, however, the need for routine was much clearer. My older child needed to be fed and play and have time for sleep at predictable times. And when I saw how essential it was for her to have routines respected, I also realized it was pretty important for us parents too.

So now I am very pro routines! But when it comes to babies, we need to be gentle about them. It is as if we are saying, 'Welcome! This is how we do things here, and I know it will take you a bit of time to get used to it.' So I would always feed a baby that was hungry, or let one sleep that was tired. With my son I made an effort to establish an early bedtime from the earliest weeks, and

I did what I could to keep him asleep for the whole evening. Often that meant me going to bed at 6 p.m. too, so I could lie next to him!

You sometimes hear babycare experts advocating routines as part of a package to make babies more manageable and independent. It's true that routines and rituals make babies feel more secure, so it's up to you if you want to use them to support your baby to become more independent. At this stage, I think it's unrealistic to expect your baby to be happy spending much time apart from you, so I don't emphasize that aspect of routines. And some babycare experts suggest routines that are so strict parents aren't even allowed to leave the house at certain times of the day. I think this is going too far.

Instead, my rule of thumb is that routines are there to *serve the needs of the family*, and not the family serving the needs of the routine!

MINDFULLY HOLDING A CRYING BABY

A friend recently reminded me of a beautiful teaching: when we feel difficult emotions in ourselves, such as anger, we should try to hold these emotions with mindfulness, just as a mother tenderly holds her crying baby. I think this is a really lovely image, and for me it immediately evokes qualities of patience, compassion and acceptance.

The comparison works because it relies upon an archetypal image of the mother as the embodiment of gentleness and under-standing. I think that most parents will recognize this experience, and be able to recall incidences of it. However, I also think this teaching is a little dangerous, because it idealizes motherhood/parenthood.

Sometimes it is *really* difficult to hold a crying baby. Crying babies can wear down our patience and make us feel impotent. Perhaps your baby has been crying for hours. Or perhaps she just started crying but it's the final straw in an otherwise stressful day.

Perhaps nothing will soothe her. Perhaps it's the middle of the night and you are so desperate for sleep that you feel like vomiting. You may be frightened that she will never stop, or that she is ill, or that the neighbours will hear and judge you. You may feel like you have failed. Instead of holding your baby tenderly, your arms are tense and your movements fraught. Although you may still be saying 'hush', the words are said through clenched teeth. You may begin to feel angry with your baby.

The truth is that parents do not always know how to hold their babies. And when I say *hold*, I don't just mean the physical act of carrying them or cuddling them, I also mean hold on a deeper psychological level. I mean *allowing* her to speak out her emotions – whether those are positive or negative – and accepting that communication without criticism. Sometimes this comes easily and naturally to us. At other times it feels impossible. However, I think that we can learn how to hold our babies mindfully.

UNDERSTANDING OUR ROLE AND RESPONSIBILITIES

Many parents get into difficulty because they believe that it is their job to keep their baby happy. But that is a misunderstanding. It's our job as parents to do our best to meet our baby's needs. But that's not the same as keeping them happy (or quiet). Of course, babies are more likely to be happy when their needs are being met. But the two are quite separate things. The only person responsible for your baby's emotions is your baby. When she is expressing her feelings, it's your job to listen.

We need to develop the quality of *equanimity* in order to allow our baby to take responsibility for her own happiness. Equanimity is a state of composure, balance and groundedness, which helps us to accept and allow reality as it is. By not resisting reality, we can forge deeper empathic connections. Of course, this doesn't just apply to parenting a baby – equanimity nourishes us in all our relationships. I discuss this in much more depth in Chapter 4.

My son had silent reflux and screamed all the time unless he was being nursed. We could not put him down, and he barely slept. It was so hard to hear his crying. I tried to bring awareness to my body and his when he was on the breast and nursing, as this was the time when he was quiet and settled. I was so grateful that I would attend to his features and smell and that would help me reconnect in a loving way to him.

Emily, mum to Owen, 2

LETTING YOUR BABY CRY

Now I absolutely don't mean ignore your baby. We know from scientific research and our own gut feeling that leaving babies to cry alone has a negative impact on their emotional development. What I am saying is that we must *allow* our babies to cry when they need to. We shouldn't be *afraid* of their crying.

In the main, babies cry to communicate that they are having an unpleasant experience. This experience is typically triggered by something that's not quite right in their world. Perhaps they are feeling the first growls of hunger, or they have pins and needles, or a stomachache. Or they are overtired or over-stimulated. Often it's possible for us parents to do something to set the world to rights. We can feed our baby or cuddle her, or take her for a walk to help settle her to sleep. Once she is relieved from her negative experience, she is free to stop crying and return to contentedness.

So as parents we start to build up a picture that crying equals bad parenting. Rather than thinking, *Am I doing all I can to meet my baby's needs?* We start to think: *What can I do to stop the crying?* The trouble with this is that there will come times when you *can't* make things better for your baby. Perhaps she has a fever or a pain in her stomach or is just so wound up that she can't drift off into the sleep she desperately needs.

The parent who mindfully allows a baby to cry probably doesn't look much different to the parent who is trying to stop a baby crying. Both parents – let's say fathers – comfort their babies through holding, rocking and singing soothing songs. The difference is on the inside. The father who is allowing his baby to cry is relaxed and compassionate. He doesn't worry whether the crying will continue or stop. 'I know you're feeling sad,' he might murmur in her ear. 'I'll keep on holding you.'

The father who is trying to stop his baby from crying, however, feels tense and agitated. Perhaps he is caught up in his baby's drama, overwhelmed by the distress of the situation. Or he may feel angry that his baby is not responding to his efforts to soothe her. He may feel disempowered and judged.

The irony is that the baby held by the mindful father is far more likely to calm down quicker. Babies are empathic creatures who respond to our internal state. So being relaxed and accepting about our babies' distress is much more likely to soothe them.

Of course a young baby hardly even knows that she is crying or what it is about, let alone what you the parent is feeling. But over time, if we continue to be frightened of, or averse to our babies' difficult feelings, then we begin to send them unintentional messages. First we begin to teach them that unhappiness is something to be afraid of and got rid of as quickly as possible. We may start to set up patterns of always looking for a distraction or new stimulation whenever unhappiness starts to surface. Our negative reaction to their crying may send them a signal that we are not prepared to accept them in all of their states. Simply put this translates to: we like you better when you are happy.

Now this is probably very far from the truth – perhaps you are motivated to stop the crying simply because you find it so hard to see your baby unhappy. It is often the parents who are most responsive and loving to their babies that feel the greatest sense of failure when their baby is unhappy.

I fell into this trap when my first child was a baby. I was determined to meet her every need. I fed her on demand, day and night, barely ever put her down, and was determined to understand the reason behind every single grimace or murmur. So when she cried and I couldn't stop it, I felt utterly hopeless. When my son was born I learnt to apply my mindfulness practice to his cries. When he was in distress, I tried hard to listen to him, and to let him know with the way I held him that he was heard. I remember him being ill with a fever at only a few weeks old and knowing that there was nothing practical I could do for him. I can still now recall that feeling of spaciousness and acceptance that I felt as I comforted and rocked him in the night.

TIP: When crying is too difficult to bear

Although mindfully holding and listening may be the ideal response to a crying baby, there can be times when this isn't possible. It may be that unresolved issues from your own childhood make it more difficult to accept your baby's tears. Or it could be that circumstances in the present – such as exhaustion, or too many demands, prevent you from listening calmly. Whatever the reason, if you find yourself getting angry or stressed with your baby, then acknowledge this to yourself with kindness.

If you can, ask someone to take over for a while – your partner, or a neighbour or a friend. If no one is around to help you, then leaving your baby in a safe place for a few moments while you take a breather – perhaps in another room or in the garden – may help you to feel more grounded. Do something for yourself, such as go to the loo or wash your face. Sharing your feelings with friends, family, or perhaps a counsellor, can help you to feel more supported.

When babies grow a little older, it becomes clear that some crying is unavoidable. In fact, in our role as teachers to our children, we will often cause those tears ourselves. As inquisitive older babies and toddlers become more experimental, parents often have to thwart them in their desires. But we can do that kindly, while accepting the fact that our limits are causing them distress. If we don't fear their tears, then we can make wiser decisions about how we guide their behaviour. Learning how to lovingly accept their tears in babyhood will stand you in good stead for the challenges ahead.

Mindfully accepting when your baby is crying and unhappy is also a powerful gift you can give her. Because ultimately you are teaching her that it's OK to be unhappy – her feelings are valid. We can be with that unhappiness, and watch it, and, when it's ready, allow it to pass. This is setting the foundations for your child's ability to be mindful about her feelings as she grows up.

SUMMARY

- *All parents want to get to know their new babies. This is a very natural time for mindfulness to arise, as you look so closely and without judgement at the new being in your arms.*
- *A new baby brings a change to the pace of life. This can be liberating as you start to pay more attention to the smaller things. It can also be challenging, as you let go of your usual distractions.*
- *Babies cause a huge amount of chaos, which makes it extremely difficult to maintain a formal practice in the early weeks. Gently guiding your baby toward a routine that meets everyone's needs may help.*
- *It's not our job to keep babies happy, or to stop them from crying. It's up to us to meet their needs and listen to the expression of their feelings.*
- *Mindfully allowing our babies to cry prevents us from getting overwhelmed. It also demonstrates to our babies that we love them in all their guises, and ultimately helps them to tolerate their own challenging feelings.*

4

Developing Positive Qualities

When we practise mindfulness we start to see each other as we really are. This can enable us to become more connected with ourselves and those around us. But if we just practised bare attention without any warmth it might lead to indifference. In order to develop our relationships, we need to incorporate other positive qualities of connection.

Buddhism teaches that there are four qualities that we can develop on a foundation of mindfulness:

- loving-kindness
- compassion
- joy
- equanimity

We need these four attitudes in order to achieve harmonious and fulfilling connections with others. It is when they slip away that conflict and suffering arise. These qualities play such an important part in the family. We are probably closer to our children than we are, or will ever be, with any other person. And the quality of that relationship will shape the way your child develops and interacts with the world as they grow. Therefore, maintaining a loving, empathic approach will not only bring you both joy and happiness right now, but it will also enable your child to have a greater resource of empathy to draw on in later life.

But that's not to say that you are stuck with the quota of love that your parents gave you as a child. Nothing in life is fixed. When we become conscious of our choices, we find that our capacity to grow is unlimited. Just like mindfulness, the four qualities can actually be *cultivated*. This means that if we practise them, we can actually feel *more* love, *more* joy, *more* compassion, and *more* equanimity. We can make the feelings themselves stronger and more consistent. This will have immediate and long-lasting benefits for you and your children.

We can learn how to extend the feelings beyond our immediate circle. This enriches our relationships by bringing happiness to both ourselves and others, and, by developing these qualities, we also push at the limits that hold us back and increase our own capacity for love and happiness.

LOVING COMES NATURALLY TO PARENTS

Becoming a parent gives us a massive head start on cultivating these qualities. Biology, hormones, instinct and culture all play their part in setting us up to feel empathic toward our children. It comes naturally to us. When we hold our baby in our arms and feel an uncomplicated, unconditional love, that feeling is loving-kindness.

It may be the first time you have experienced loving-kindness in its pure form – without any neediness, or yearning, or expectations or requirements. We don't worry whether or not the love is returned. Our baby doesn't have to smile, or coo, or open his eyes. We love him however he is.

Feeling these emotions tends to leave us ripe for increasing empathy more generally – not just toward our children, but also more widely. This is why being a parent gives us such a great start in cultivating these empathic qualities. Not only are we given the gift of feeling love toward our own child, but we are also predisposed to develop it. In the rest of this chapter, I will explore the four qualities of loving-kindness, compassion, joy and equanimity in more depth and explain how they relate to one another. I'll also discuss how we can set about increasing our capacity for them.

Being a parent reminds me that experiences we have are the building blocks for following experiences. Having children reminds me that adults, like children, absorb kind experiences and build upon them.
Kate, mum to Zach, 2½

LOVING-KINDNESS

Loving-kindness is the same as love, though in our culture the word *love* has many shades of meaning. The love I mean here is not a yearning, needy kind of love, but one that replenishes both giver and receiver. It doesn't ask for anything in return. At one end of the spectrum it's a feeling of warmth and well-wishing just as we might feel toward our friends, on the other end it's an intense, transcendent love that embodies and resonates from our whole being.

I have already said that we have a natural tendency to feel loving-kindness toward our children. However, this feeling may not stay intact forever. In fact, it definitely won't! Inevitably, moments of conditionality creep in to our love for our children; times when we wish they would stop crying, be less clingy, more polite or in some other way different to how they actually are. By making a commitment to practising loving-kindness, we can learn to support, consolidate and maintain our loving feelings toward our children.

DEVELOPING LOVING-KINDNESS TOWARD OURSELVES

Cultivating loving-kindness toward others goes hand in hand with developing it toward ourselves. It's as if our soul is a mirror: the loving-kindness that we can accept on our own behalf can be reflected back into the wider world. If there is just an empty black hole where the mirror should be, then we won't have as many resources at our disposal to send love to others. In that case we

MEDITATION PRACTICE:
How to develop loving-kindness toward ourselves

At first it may seem awkward directing loving-kindness toward yourself. The task is to bring together the sense of well-wishing with an awareness of yourself. Start by directing your attention inward, so that you can find yourself in your body. It's important to notice who you are *right now*. Noticing physical sensations in your body can help you do this.

The traditional way to develop loving-kindness in meditation is by silently repeating the phrase: 'May I be well and happy and free from suffering.' You can change the wording to something that really resonates with you. 'May I be free from strain and stress. May I be at ease. May I be content.'

Sometimes the words can feel empty. It may take many times of trying the exercise before any feeling is conjured. Another way to call up loving-kindness is to use some kind of visualization. Imagine the warmth spreading around and through you as if you are in a sauna. Or that the loving feeling is a warm, drizzling rain that gradually soaks through your clothes into your skin. Some people find it helpful to bring to mind a benevolent person, perhaps the Buddha or Jesus, or someone more personal to you. Imagine the warmth and love radiating from them toward you. It could be in the form of golden beads that move along a thread into your heart.

The point I am trying to make here with all these suggestions, is that it's absolutely fine for you to play around and find out what works for you. Just like with mindfulness, you can do this exercise either formally or informally. It can be done while sitting quietly, perhaps with eyes closed, for a certain length of time, or it can be done at any moment you remember, perhaps while walking down the street, or while looking out the window.

may feel that loving our children takes up all of our energy, and we don't have anything left for others. Or we may even find it hard to feel loving toward them, especially when they (or we) are tired and grumpy.

FINDING IT DIFFICULT TO DEVELOP LOVING-KINDNESS INWARD

At times when I have found it difficult to direct loving-kindness toward myself, I have worried that means I can't love my children properly or be a positive entity in the world. This triggers feelings of inadequacy and failure, which make it even harder to find loving-kindness for myself. Of course this is not helpful!

What I have come to realize is that we don't necessarily need to develop loving-kindness toward ourselves and then to others in a rigid sequence. That might suggest that the love we feel toward others is somehow not valid, unless we feel sure we have already directed it toward ourselves. As I already said, the two go hand in hand. As we develop one, we develop the other. The trick is to notice this as it happens, so that loving-kindness directed outward supports loving-kindness directed inward, and vice versa.

So if you are finding it hard to recognize the feeling toward yourself, but you are very conscious of the warmth you feel toward your baby (for example) then spend some time dwelling in that feeling of love. Allow it to grow and spread and, when you feel ready, allow yourself to 'dip' into it too. In fact, you are already there – you just don't necessarily know it. Don't start overthinking it. The concept of 'directional' loving-kindness may even be unhelpful. If negative or confusing thoughts arise, simply return to the feeling of loving-kindness toward your baby. This kind of pure love for others replenishes us too, so as long as we know that, we can begin to nurture our feelings of warmth and acceptance toward ourselves.

DIRECTING LOVING-KINDNESS OUTWARD

Once we are familiar with the feeling of loving-kindness, then we become more confident in the way we can conjure it up and direct it. We can learn to amplify it by recognizing it, valuing it and calling it up – whenever we remember.

This enables us to both enjoy and increase the love we already feel for those we care for. We can make it stronger, more consistent and longer lasting. This means we can deepen and strengthen our relationships with our family. Instead of allowing our children to become disconnected as they inevitably grow more independent from us, we forge a strong bond that reminds us to reconnect. Loving-kindness urges us to try to understand our children better, and this understanding in turn leads to acceptance and more love.

> Previously when I was angry or harsh with my kids, once the anger evaporated I would be awash with toxic levels of guilt, self-criticism, shame and sadness that would further impair my ability to parent skilfully. Being more accepting and non-judgemental of times when I don't do a great job makes it much quicker and easier to repair what went wrong.
>
> *Guin, MBCP meditation teacher and mum of three*

Another way to extend the range of our warm feelings is to direct the quality to different people, in this order: to ourselves, to someone who helps us (e.g. a teacher/mentor/role model), a good friend, someone neutral, someone we find challenging.

It can feel very difficult at first to sustain our feeling of loving-kindness once we have brought to mind someone difficult. At first it may be better not to choose *the most* difficult person in your life. Save them till you have done a bit more practice!

But noticing the reluctance to wish that person well can teach us a lot about our limitations. Whenever we feel that stickiness, it shows us exactly where we are being held back. Try to examine what that feeling is. It may be fear that opening ourselves up to that person will leave us vulnerable or diminished. If we can be very mindful and honest about our feelings, then we may be able to allow ourselves – very gently – to be open and accepting to that person too. And this may have very different consequences to what we feared.

MEDITATION PRACTICE:
Extending the circle and limits of loving-kindness

We can also learn to direct our goodwill toward people outside of our immediate circle. Again, this can be done in formal meditation, straight after sending loving-kindness inward. Start by sending the loving feeling to other people or creatures in the room where you sit. Then include the whole building. Radiate outward so that your love expands to include the neighbourhood. Now extend it to the town or city. Widen your circle to include the country. And the continent. And now the entire world . . . and beyond.

COMPASSION

Compassion is a form of love. It's what happens naturally when our loving-kindness looks upon someone who is suffering. Compassion is often confused with pity, but the two are quite different. When we pity, we protect ourselves by keeping separate. We look down on the person in pain and stay disconnected. Compassion, however, comes from *sharing* suffering. We recognize pain, and we allow ourselves to feel it too. This is what makes us wince when we see a child fall down and scrape his knee.

It can be difficult to feel compassion, because that means admitting pain. This can be scary for both children and adults. If the child who has fallen over is our own child, we may feel a sense of urgency to try to put things right. It is common to see parents distracting children, 'Oh! Look at that flower' or ascribing blame, 'What a naughty rock for tripping you over.' They may deny the sensation: 'Come on, that didn't hurt!' Or even feel angry: 'I keep telling you to be careful!'

However, all of these responses miss the opportunity for practising compassion. Even saying, 'Let me kiss it better' can be a way of trying to avoid the pain.

Giving your child a cuddle and saying either in words or in a look, 'Yes, I know that hurt,' allows you both to face up to and share the pain. This is one way to embrace compassion. It teaches our children that pain can be tolerated, and they'll find out for themselves that it doesn't last.

Practising compassion with our children in this way can be very healing. It can give them the confidence to deal with suffering. Because we are acknowledging them as they really are in that moment, these repeated experiences of quiet compassion are incredibly affirming and validating. They give us a chance to deepen our connection.

It doesn't make any difference whether the pain is physical or psychological. When children are denied the chance to experience their own pain, they may hang onto it all the harder – prolonging their grievance or crying or wound cradling. Or, if the parent responds by leaping in to make everything better, children may draw out the drama to enjoy the special flurry of attention. Simple compassionate holding teaches our children to be mindful at challenging moments. By staying quiet and not hurrying our children to feel better, we can allow them the chance to decide for themselves when the pain has passed. They will probably surprise you by moving on quickly. In essence, we are empowering our children to be responsible for their own happiness.

FEELING COMPASSION FOR OURSELVES

The idea of feeling compassion for ourselves may seem unfamiliar at first. We may feel we don't deserve it – that it would be self-indulgent. But I'm not suggesting that we revel in self-pity or feeling sorry for ourselves, perhaps by repeating stories to ourselves about how we have been mistreated or whatever.

Compassion for ourselves means acknowledging and allowing ourselves to be in pain when we find it, and holding that pain carefully in our hands, perhaps in the way we might hold a trembling rabbit. I find that the easiest way to check for suffering in myself is to scan through my body looking for any tightness or discomfort. This seems to work for psychological pain too, as it also manifests itself in the body. If I detect tension or strain, I try to allow myself to feel that pain, perhaps by breathing into it. Sitting quietly with suffering takes much of the fear out of the experience. Denying it can cause us more suffering.

DIRECTING COMPASSION OUTWARD

Just as with loving-kindness, we can work on expanding our sphere of compassion to include more and more people. This doesn't necessarily mean rushing over and quietly holding every child in the playground that grazes a knee. That may not be appropriate. Instead I mean simply allowing yourself to share in the suffering of others when you come across it.

Compassionate feeling *may* be followed by action or it may not. It may mean donating to a good cause or sending a sympathy card; it may be simply allowing yourself to be touched. You may wonder what the point of compassion is, if it doesn't lead to action. If we practise feeling compassion even when it doesn't seem possible to help in a practical way, then we are preparing ourselves to be ready when opportunities to help *do* arise. The important thing is that you are allowing yourself to be receptive to suffering – at any time. Suffering is an inherent part of our reality. If we turn away from it and deny it, then we are necessarily living in a kind of pretence. And if our illusion is threatened, we can feel scared and undermined. As the Czech writer Franz Kafka put it: 'You can hold yourself back from the sufferings of the world, that is something you are free to do and it accords with your nature, but perhaps this very holding back is the one suffering you could avoid.'

———————

It has made me feel more compassionate toward my own parents, and more grateful, as I see what they went through to bring us up, how tough it can be and how generous they were with us. It's encouraged me to 'look deeply' into my parents' own upbringings as well, to see how the difficulties they had as children has led to certain behaviours in them as adults. When you see the root causes of why people behave as they do, it's much easier to be compassionate and to forgive them. There is a wonderful meditation where you see your parents as a five-year-old child, what they were going through then. It's very healing.

Ben, dad to Leo, 6

———————

JOY

Just as love turns to compassion when it finds suffering, love naturally manifests as joy when it looks upon happiness. When we love people, we celebrate their successes. This feeling is also called *sympathetic joy*, because it is about sharing joy with others. It is said that this is the hardest of the four qualities to develop. Unless we have a high degree of loving-kindness toward the person experiencing success, we can feel resentful or jealous, as if their joy somehow diminishes our own. Luckily, parents have an abundance of opportunities to practise sympathetic joy, and a predisposition to find it easy. Of course, we expect to experience delight at the big milestones: our baby's first steps, his first word, the first time he rides a bike. But actually, when we look more closely, we can and do share our children's joy many times a day.

DEVELOPING JOY

Making a conscious effort to develop joy may feel a bit frivolous. Surely it's not as important as love or compassion? Check within yourself to see whether you have this hesitancy. It could indicate that you need to develop more loving-kindness toward yourself. We all want to be happy. That's why we pursue a path such as a mindfulness practice. Developing joy does exactly that – it helps us to be happier. It helps other people to be happy too.

The great news is that joy doesn't run out. Sharing our own and other people's joy *multiplies* it. The more we look for opportunities to feel joy, the more we have it. As the Dalai Lama points out, if we can share other people's joy as well as just our own, we increase our chances of happiness billions of times over.[7]

TIP: Noticing and sharing joy

A good way to approach this practice is to start where it's easy. Look for times when your child is happy or has had some small achievement. You won't have to look far – it happens all the time! Simply notice the sensation of gladness within you as you share in that joy. Sharing this moment again with someone else who finds it easy to care for your child, such as grandma or your partner, can also spread the joy further.

Thich Nhat Hanh makes an important point about happiness. He says that we have a tendency to fix on one idea of happiness. When that doesn't go to plan, we close the door to any other sources of happiness.[8] I think this type of scenario can come up so frequently with children. Say, for example, you are trying to put your two-year-old son to bed, but he is resisting bedtime. You lie down next to him, desperate for the moment when he closes his eyes to sleep, and you can clock off. However, instead of dozing off, now he is climbing over you, sliding out of the bed and toddling to the door. He gives you a cheeky wave as he pushes it open and disappears from view. It may be that you are so fixed on the idea that his being asleep will bring you happiness, that you can't see he is being rather funny and cute. If you allow yourself to be open to a different kind of happiness than the one you had planned for, you may be pleasantly surprised. Perhaps he will return with a teddy bear to tuck *you* in to bed, or some other endearing antic, and so create a memory you'll cherish for years.

WHEN DEVELOPING JOY IS DIFFICULT

Sharing in joy when our loving-kindness is not so strong can be harder, and it's especially difficult to share the joy of those that we find challenging, or that are causing harm to others. Instead of being glad at their successes, we begrudge them and may feel angry or resentful. We may even want to see them punished. Try to observe this stickiness in yourself when it comes up. Bringing mindfulness to bear on it helps us become a little softer. Recognize that we all want to be happy, and, without being self-critical, gently probe why you would deny somebody that chance. Perhaps you are afraid that feeling generous toward someone you dislike would somehow damage your identity or your beliefs.

In the past, when I was less sure of myself and what I was doing, I often found that other people's achievements left me feeling inadequate. I avoided looking on social media because I found it painful to hear about friends' career successes, holidays or house purchases. It wasn't so much that I resented their good fortune – in theory I was pleased for them. But in practice it was hard for me to move beyond my own feelings of failure to actually share in their happiness. If this sounds familiar, it may mean that you are not directing enough loving-kindness toward yourself. I found that when I started accepting myself for who and what I was, I stopped comparing myself to others so much. I also started to make more positive choices in my life, which led to my own successes, which in turn made me more confident and able to be happy for others.

In fact developing loving-kindness to others and ourselves may be an easier way to approach joy – as it will naturally turn to joy when it finds good fortune. Just be sure to notice that you are not limiting yourself by offering your love selectively. Perhaps you find it easy to feel compassion when your friend suffers hard times, but when she has good luck, you disconnect. The change of fortunes could even make you feel rejected. Being mindful about what's going on – especially when we come up against our limits, can help us to move beyond them. By opening our hearts to joy wherever it appears, we are greatly expanding our own capacity to feel happiness.

EQUANIMITY

When I talked about compassion, I gave the example of a child grazing his knee in the playground (see page 47). When it's our own child our reaction may be to deny, distract or make it better. However, it can be so much easier to feel simple compassion when the child is not our own. When we don't feel responsible, we are more able to accept the reality for what it is, and allow our empathy to arise. This feeling of balance is what is meant by equanimity.

I like to think of loving-kindness as a tree that grows up and reaches out into the world, with compassion and joy as branches of that tree. Equanimity is the root system that steadies and sustains it. Without equanimity our tree would be parched by the hot sun and knocked down by the wind.

Equanimity is the quality that enables us to continue to love and feel compassion and joy, even when it's difficult. Perhaps our love is not returned, or suffering seems too painful to bear. Equanimity protects us, by keeping us balanced and grounded. It reminds us that even though we do what we can to be kind and helpful, we cannot *make* people happy. They have to do that for themselves. Equanimity allows us to love without an agenda, feel compassion without slipping into despair, feel joy without clinging.

TIP: Noticing equanimity

As with the other three qualities, the best way to start is by noticing the feeling when equanimity is obvious. It often manifests as a kind of calm solidity perhaps even amidst some kind of trouble. Once you have got familiar with it, it is much easier to conjure it up. You may be able to increase it simply by reminding yourself about it. I used to think that success was about staying in control. However, as a parent I began to realize that being able to relinquish control reveals a much greater power. Equanimity is about letting go of outcomes and agendas and allowing things to be as they are. Although at first glance this may seem like passivity, in fact this conscious choice is extremely empowering.

CULTIVATING EQUANIMITY

The classic way of cultivating equanimity is to acknowledge that each person is in charge of his or her own happiness. This can be incredibly difficult to accept as a parent! I already touched on this idea when I talked about holding a crying baby in Chapter 3 (see page 36). Yes, we have a responsibility to try to meet our children's needs, but that is not the same thing as keeping them happy. For a start, it would be impossible to keep them free from pain. Believing it's our responsibility can actually be harmful for both our children and us. If we always act as if we are the only people who can make things better for our children when times are tough, then this undermines their ability to tolerate pain and to choose to let go of unnecessary suffering. And we are setting ourselves up for failure if we aim for such an impossible ideal.

WHEN NEEDS HAVE TO BE COMPROMISED

When you have just one child, it is not so hard to respond to his needs quickly and consistently. Trusting in your child and being a responsive parent helps children gain confidence and become emotionally secure. But you may find that you have a tendency to put everything on hold for him – forgoing your own nourishment so that you can feed your baby, missing out on your shower, cancelling social engagements and so on. A certain amount of this is inevitable. However, having a second child quickly throws up all sorts of issues about conflicting needs and compromise. Times of conflict are where equanimity comes in especially useful.

At bedtime, the day after my son was born, I lay down with my daughter to help her go to sleep, as was our custom. But as I lay there, I heard my newborn son start to cry. I was absolutely torn – should I rush to him, or should I stay here with my daughter, who seemed on the cusp of sleep? I wanted to protect her feelings at a time of great upheaval. I made the choice to stay, and let my new baby cry in the arms of his dad for a few minutes.

But as soon as I was able to get to him and start to feed him, I knew that I had made the wrong decision. On this occasion, his need was greater than hers. At that moment I saw that I needed to take a different approach to meeting the children's needs and that it was never again going to be a simple matter of 'putting my child first'.

But the interesting thing was that as my children grew, I saw that, in fact, it wasn't necessarily such a good thing for the children to have their needs met instantly, all the time. Inevitably there would be times when the children would have to make sacrifices for each other. One child might have to interrupt his deep play in order to take another child to a swimming lesson, say. Or the baby might have to wait for a feed while I helped his sister in the bathroom.

Although I might prioritize the really basic needs – to be fed and to have time to sleep – even these had to give way to a more pressing urgent need at times. And, of course, the less obvious needs, such as the need to play in a self-directed way, or the need to experience winning a race, or the need to have a cuddle, would often have to be put on hold or curtailed in some way. I began to understand that striking a balance meant assessing urgency in the moment, and also keeping in mind an overview. For example, although generally feeding my baby son might take precedence over reading a story to his older sister, there may be occasions when the reverse is true. Perhaps when his sister is unwell, or is upset, or the end of the story is only a page away. Or her story has been interrupted by a feed every night this last week.

I realized that the decisions I took may not be right for everyone, every time, but as long as each child could be *generally* confident that their needs were being mostly met, then I was providing a safe enough structure for them to experience disappointments. I began to see that being able to experience disappointments, and learning to tolerate them, is a need in itself. I believe that this, (along with maintaining the positive boundaries that I discuss in Chapter 8) builds the foundations of equanimity for your child.

You don't need to have two or more children in order to appreciate this point – it's clear that we ought to take into account the needs of parents and wider society, even when we only have one child. However, having more than one child certainly brings the point home.

WHEN EQUANIMITY IS DIFFICULT

At times, equanimity can be very difficult. When we feel very strongly about someone, and feel close to them, we can lose our perspective. This can happen very easily with our children. It's so easy to get caught up in their dramas, whether that's frustration or anger or sorrow. Equanimity, and especially the lack of it, can be contagious, and unfortunately children have very little of their own. This makes it both harder, and all the more important, for us to maintain it ourselves.

Equanimity means accepting circumstances that are beyond our control, and yet staying connected. We may find ourselves feeling angry and frustrated, wishing things were different. In these circumstances, I think that the most helpful way to nurture equanimity is to try to understand why things are the way they are. This can help us see and accept reality as it is. But that's not always possible. Sometimes we just have to accept that things are not the way we would choose, even if we don't know why.

WHEN EQUANIMITY IS ESPECIALLY IMPORTANT

Equanimity becomes especially important when we turn our attention to a person we find particularly challenging. It may be that this is someone you love, who is rejecting you. Or it may be someone who is causing suffering elsewhere. Sometimes we may think we ought to feel compassion for troubling people – ruthless dictators, for example, may have had very hard upbringings, or some other source of unhappiness that they perpetuate.

I think it can be very difficult to feel compassion when the person themselves is not aware of their own pain. It is hard to share their pain, if they don't seem to be experiencing it. In these cases equanimity becomes the most appropriate quality to try to cultivate.

Equanimity is not indifference. It does not turn away: it gives us the strength to look for longer and more deeply. It may be that by exploring more deeply, we are eventually able to feel compassion for the person who is causing suffering. Equanimity underpins the other three qualities, enabling them to go further outward. Without it we would have a very hard time sustaining our empathy.

CHILDREN CONNECT US TO HUMANITY

Many new parents are bowled over by the enormous amount of loving-kindness, compassion and joy that they suddenly feel for the little being who has come into their lives. For a while we may be wholly taken up with the small trials and achievements of our little one.

By observing our own child so closely, we start to understand how everything he does is a culmination of everything that has gone before. At first we know the origin of every single word he utters, we recognize gestures and facial expressions that he has picked up from the people around him. We know that he is crotchety because he has woken early from a nap. After a while, however, his environment gets larger and many more things influence him, until we can no longer pick out why he has used a particular expression or what made him suddenly grumpy when we picked him up from nursery. But we can still understand that he is acting in a certain way for a reason, and this understanding greatly enables us to love and accept him for who he is.

It is quite natural then, for parents to begin to look outward at some time or another, and begin to see that what is true for their own child, is also true for every other child. And, indeed for every adult who was once a child. And we remember that all people were children once, with mothers and fathers who loved *them*. In this way I think that loving a child can act as a template for the way we interact with the wider world. It connects us to the whole of humanity.

Around the time my daughter was born my empathy surged upward, so that I felt others' suffering much more keenly. I remember specifically struggling with what to do about strong compassion for children orphaned by war. Moving to equanimity can stop such thoughts becoming overwhelming, but I feel an ethical imperative to do what I can . . . It also leads me to think about how my immediate day-to-day actions can help to avoid any suffering for my wife and daughter too.

Ed, dad to Ruth, 9

SUMMARY

- *In order to have positive relationships, we need to cultivate empathy alongside mindfulness. The four empathic qualities are loving-kindness, compassion, joy and equanimity.*

- *Being a parent gives us a massive head start, as we are naturally inclined to feel empathic and have plenty of opportunities to practise.*
- *Loving-kindness is an unconditional love that we can develop by familiarizing ourselves with it and calling it up.*
- *Loving-kindness turns to compassion when it finds pain, and joy when it finds happiness.*
- *Equanimity sustains and stabilizes us as we reach outward. It enables us to remain unruffled by events beyond our control.*

5

Mindful Parenting, Day by Day

A friend of mine recently told me about the time when she first applied mindfulness to parenting. She was seeing a therapist who suggested she spend 10 minutes each day playing mindfully with her toddler.

I started thinking about the way I read to him. I read to him a lot, but all the time I'm not with him – I'm actually thinking about dinner or the chores I've got to do next, or wondering how long it will take him to get to sleep. When I started reading mindfully, I realized how exciting it must be for him – hearing and seeing that story, finding out what happens next. And I started sharing in his delight and excitement too. And then I felt sad that I had never read to him in that way before. But I was also glad that he was still young, and we had many more opportunities to read books together.

Kate, mum to Zach, 2½

Perhaps the most important thing about parenting with mindfulness is the depth of the connection forged between you and your child during mindful moments.

Research shows that this type of shared attention is fundamental to children's social, emotional and cognitive development.[9]

Once we have made a commitment to be more mindful throughout our day, we can work toward trying to be mindful *all the time*. However, I don't think it's terribly helpful to simply leave it at that. In this chapter I'll look at some very typical everyday circumstances, in order to explore ideas about how mindfulness might work in practice.

JOINING YOUR CHILD IN PLAY

The importance and the power of connected play was really brought home to me in Lawrence J. Cohen's book *Playful Parenting*.[10] Cohen shows that play is children's way of learning about and processing the world. Self-directed play – that is, playing without interference, empowers children to navigate the world with confidence and joy. That is not to say we should *never* steer our children's play. Cohen gives plenty of examples of how we can transform destructive disconnecting play into an opportunity to make a connection.

There are many different theories about the best ways to spend time with children. Some people stress the importance of *quality time* with their children – perhaps earmarking specific periods in the week for playing and being together. Others rate *quantity* more highly – considering parental availability to be the most important thing – even when parents don't necessarily have their full attention on their child. Some people provide a very child-centred environment, where the activities of the day revolve around the child's interests; others prefer to 'bring their children along' in a more adult environment.

Of course, all of these different approaches to parenting will influence the way the child grows and develops. But there is no one *right way* to do things. I would go so far as to say that strict adherence to any one specific child-rearing philosophy could leave you in danger of missing the reality of what *your* child needs *at this moment*.

Mindful connection with your child is a very important part of discerning those needs. And engaging with your child in play is an excellent way to establish that connection. Whether that's for a prolonged period a couple of times a week, or simply a few seconds of exchange many times a day, these moments of connection allow us to really experience the world from our children's perspective. When we allow ourselves to be drawn into our children's fantasy worlds, we are being given an opportunity to glimpse into their inner world. Through play, children explore their fears and frustrations, and their triumphs and desires.

When we bring mindfulness to our playtime with our children, we make a commitment to staying with their game. When we notice our attention wandering off to the next set of chores we need to do, we can choose to bring our attention back to the matter at hand. Instead of resenting the activity, or feeling bored or frustrated, we can allow ourselves to settle into the game and begin to enjoy it. Without mindfulness, we may not even be aware that our attention has wandered, and we may not be aware that this very moment is providing us with the potential to re-establish a bond with our child.

By deliberately or intuitively putting myself in the present I can apply the habits I've developed through meditation to focus on the playing. In this way, we can share the experience of a flow activity, which she perhaps finds easier to get absorbed in, making it more enjoyable for both of us and bringing us closer.

Ed, dad to Ruth, 9

RE-ESTABLISHING CONNECTION

So often, when I have a day with nothing particular planned, I'll opt to stay at home with the hope that my children will amuse themselves while I get on with some chores or work. And sometimes this is necessary. Chores and work do need to be done. But I think there can be a tendency to look for this type of work as a defence against really being in the moment with our children.

We persuade ourselves that it's top priority, not realizing that it has become an avoidance strategy.

Making time to be mindful and connect with our children is actually one of the most important jobs we can do, yet sometimes it slips down to the bottom of the list, especially once our children are out of the very needy baby and toddler stage. As they get older, we welcome the fact that they don't need us quite so much, but at times this goes too far. We get used to them playing more independently and we resent it when they ask us for attention. Also, we can forget to build in opportunities for reconnection.

TIP: Making time for play

Earmarking special times for being together mindfully is a wonderful way to protect those times for reconnection. It may be that we need to actually schedule in certain times in the day – perhaps at bath and bedtime, or it may be some time on a weekly basis – for example, a trip to the park on a Saturday morning. Alternatively, it may be enough to just look out for opportunities to seize as and when they come along.

EATING WITH MINDFULNESS

I recently heard the saying: mindfulness is the best seasoning for any dish. By bringing awareness to our forkful of food, we can maximize our enjoyment of it. This is what we mean when we talk about *savouring* our food. What's the point of going to all the trouble of sourcing and preparing food, if we are not even aware that we are eating it? We can get to the end of a meal without having tasted a single bite.

Because we have to do it so often, eating can become a matter of refuelling – getting something inside us so we can move on to the next task. Eating with mindfulness can help us to appreciate our food all the more. It may make us more conscious of what we are putting into our bodies. That could mean considering the implications on our health, or perhaps on the wider world. Marking out times in the day when we come together to eat as a family is a great way to set the conditions for mindful eating. If we have made a special effort to come to the table at the same time, then it makes it much easier for us to be mindful while we eat. By making meals a slightly more formal occasion, they can become a celebration. Eating becomes an opportunity to reconnect with ourselves and each other. There are probably very few other times in the day when you are able to share an activity together in the same way. Ritualizing meals in some way, perhaps by expressing gratitude at the beginning or setting flowers on the table or lighting a candle, can all be ways of making meals feel more special.

Of course, it's unlikely that your mealtimes will be 'formal' in the way that meals *without* children are formal. It is very important to balance the desire to make mealtimes special with a realistic assessment of your child's stage. Insisting on staying at the table for long stretches, or eating with good manners, may simply be beyond her. Don't let your wish to make mealtimes more mindful prevent you from being mindful of who your child is right now!

We have a new practice of ringing a gong to signal it's time for everyone to come and sit down for dinner. It's much more pleasant than me shouting up the stairs 'Dinner time!' with increasing levels of irritation! Then when everyone is sitting down one of the children rings the gong again and we listen to the sound until it has completely died away before we start eating. This is a fun way to get everyone in a state of noticing their sensory experience as we begin the meal, and it also means everyone is sitting down together to eat at the same time.

Guin, MBCP meditation teacher and mum of three

USING MINDFULNESS TO PREVENT MEALTIME STRESS

For many parents, mealtimes can become a battleground, as our children refuse to eat the food we have prepared in the quantities we would like, or even at all.

If mealtimes feel like an uphill struggle, then it may be that re-establishing a mindful connection with your child can help restore some balance.

When my eldest was a baby, I read a couple of great books called *My Child Won't Eat* by Carlos Gonzales,[11] and *Baby-led Weaning* by Gill Rapley and Tracey Murkett.[12] These two books gave me confidence to trust my children to manage their own intake of food. As long as I provided my children with the opportunity to eat good food, then it wasn't my responsibility to ensure that they ate enough. They were capable of managing that for themselves. It made sense to me that, given every other animal in the world is able to regulate its own diet, the likelihood was that my animals could too.

This basis of understanding helped me to maintain equanimity (see page 53) while my children ate – or did not eat. But maintaining a mindful connection to my child in the moment was also fundamental in keeping mealtimes light and happy. By really staying aware of how my child was responding to her food, I was able to see the experience from her point of view. I could see when a helpful comment could encourage her to stay at the table for longer, and I could spot when she had really had enough and eating more would be distressing.

At mealtimes I put away my mobile phone to ignore texts,
and the desire to send any, so that we focus on the meal as
a time to enjoy food and be together.
Kate, mum to Zach, 2½

LET OUR CHILDREN TEACH US HOW TO EAT

Of course it can be annoying when children turn their nose up at a dish without even trying it, but they can sometimes teach us a great deal about how to eat. Think of a seven-month-old baby enjoying porridge for the first time. Watch how she plunges her hand into the oats, squelching and squeezing them, staring at her fingers – noticing how some grains stick to her skin, while others slowly drop off, landing splat on the table. Raising her hand to her mouth, noticing the warmth against her lips and tongue. Feeling the different textures – thick and heavy in her mouth, slight chewiness against her gums. Tasting the creaminess before swallowing and feeling the sensation of the porridge moving down the oesophagus.

Young children, especially when they try something for the first time, really immerse themselves in the experience of eating. We can use mindfulness to help us to experience eating with the same degree of focused attention.

MINDFUL CONNECTION DURING POTTY TRAINING

I've thought a great deal about potty training. With my own children I adopted the practice of baby-led potty training (BLPT), which meant that I helped them use a potty right from the earliest days. I began to run workshops in my community and later I wrote *Nappy Free Baby* all about it (see page 242).

The reason I've included it here is that I think potty training – at whatever age you approach it – provides us with a fantastic opportunity to connect with our children. Potty training is about teaching children to recognize their own bodily sensations and learn how to respond appropriately to them. But in order to anticipate when they might need to go to the toilet, and so help them take action, we need to cultivate a fine level of attunement with them. We need to become aware of their natural rhythms, so that we have a sense of when they might need to relieve themselves. To some extent we need to pick up on the little signals their bodies give us – the shifting weight from one leg to another, a glazed expression, a frenzy of activity – whatever it might be. We need to be able to detect these signs so that we can help our children learn to recognize them too.

Some parents find potty training stressful because they think they have to be on hyper-alert to their child. Often parents postpone potty training until a time when (they hope) it can be completed very quickly. But tuning into your child on this subtle level can be very rewarding. Potty training itself becomes an enjoyable process, and, much like helping a child learn to eat independently, it doesn't need to be crammed into as short a time as possible.

Remembering to tune into our children's bodies is like trying to remember to be mindful – and in fact we need a lot of mindfulness to do this job. At first it does seem like a great effort, but before long our minds get used to being aware. We find that our attention doesn't have to be absolutely focused on potty training for us to pick up on the small signals, and remember to offer it regularly. It becomes part of our way of being.

MINDFULNESS AT BEDTIME

I recently came across some words from the American writer Ralph Waldo Emerson: 'There was never a child so lovely but his mother was glad to get him to sleep.' I am sure that nature designed babies to need more hours of sleep each day, partly in order to give us parents a bit of a break.

But sometimes we can feel so desperate for those few precious hours that bedtimes themselves become a military operation, requiring every last ounce of strength and resolve.

When bedtimes are going right, they can be a nourishing and relaxing punctuation mark at the end of the day. You and your child know the routine – bath, bedtime book, nursing or perhaps a drink – however it is you do it. Bedtime routines don't require you to make complicated decisions, beyond choosing which story to read, and they provide a familiar framework for you and your child to get comfortable and cosy together. They can be a chance for you to revisit moments from earlier in the day and repackage them if necessary, or they may simply be a moment for quiet closeness.

But at other times bedtimes don't go so smoothly. Your son may be racing round the house like a maniac, getting so wound up that he bangs his head on the doorframe. Or your daughter may be resisting bedtime, dragging her feet over every stage. Bedtimes may end up getting delayed, with everyone involved getting more and more tired and fraught. Often they end in tears and tantrums.

I try very hard not to mentally whizz ahead and worry about all the chores I have to get done after lights out. If you start thinking about it then it's very easy to get cross with all the delaying tactics that kids employ at bedtime. Far better to remember that this is just the way it is at bedtime. If I stay calm and don't get cross, what seems like ages for them to settle is actually only a few minutes and then I can get to the chores.

Jan, mum to Josia, 8, and Hannah, 5

Childcare experts may promise miracle formulas for getting children off to sleep without fuss, but in most parents' experience there is no magic button. Some children find it extremely difficult to wind down to sleep. My daughter has always been one of those. As a baby I was promised that breastfeeding her would knock her out – but by about three months, it was clear that it actually took rather more effort on my part. Bedtimes regularly took a couple of hours of lying patiently beside her, calming my own breath in an effort to help her calm hers, as she wriggled and crawled and generally faffed around – until eventually sleep overcame her. At age seven, she still takes a long time to go to sleep. Her father reads her stories for the best part of an hour, and then she reads to herself for perhaps another hour after we've said goodnight.

I have found that being mindful at bedtime means being aware of my own feelings. Often I notice flickers of impatience or irritation. Noticing these feelings before I act on them means I can observe them come and go. This is not just pandering to the caprices of my child; it's being pragmatic because I know that trying to speed things up is likely to have the opposite effect. Being mindful also means noticing how important this time is for her. Perhaps it is the first time in the day when I have really been able to devote my time and attention directly to her. No wonder children like to luxuriate in it. It's so easy to get frustrated with their playfulness and see it as delaying tactics, but perhaps it is also just an invitation for us to get close to them again.

Going to sleep is also a very significant moment in the day. As babies grow into toddlers and preschoolers, they get a growing awareness of what this entails. Falling asleep is a moment of separation – from the world, the fun activities they enjoy in the day, and also from you. This is the case, even if you lie down with them while they go to sleep – even if they sleep in your room or your bed. It is still a departure from that shared consciousness.

Sleep is also a moment of letting go. Children need to learn how to let go of wakefulness and surrender to sleep. Some children seem to fear the act of falling asleep, as if the letting go of control is like a little death. It is possible that fears about the dark or about ghosts and monsters under the bed are simply ways to articulate this fear of losing control. Through time and practice, they can learn to put their faith in the going-to-sleep process. When we consider it like this, we can see how important bedtimes really are. We may need to be very sensitive about the way we handle them. Mindfulness can help us to bear these factors in mind.

SUMMARY

- *Play can be a fantastic way to deepen a mindful connection with your child. Getting down on her level allows you to see the world from her point of view*
- *Mealtimes can be an opportunity for the whole family to get together in a shared activity. Little rituals can help make them special. Remember to weigh up the needs and development stage of your children – who may not be able to sit still for long.*
- *Potty training – at whatever age – can be a way of cultivating connection. Learning how to tune into your child on a subtle, physical level can bring surprising rewards.*
- *Recognize that bedtime can be intense for parents and children. Staying mindful will help you keep aware of all of the factors involved.*

6

Keeping Things Simple

When we try to practise mindfulness in our 21st-century consumer society, in the midst of family life, we have to embrace the fact that our environment will be busy, noisy and cluttered. There's no point waiting for a miraculous calm to appear before you get started: it's not going to happen. You have to get stuck in straight away.

However, we do need to acknowledge that our environment will affect our state of mind. The busier, noisier and more cluttered it is, the more stimulated we are and the harder it is to find calm and mindfulness. So, with that in mind, it is worth taking a step back from your lifestyle and considering whether you can do more to create an environment conducive to mindfulness.

One of the things that has helped me to stay mindful in my parenting throughout the day has been simplifying the environment – it just seems to reduce the noise in my mind, making it easier to tune into my internal experience.
Guin, MBCP meditation teacher and mum of three

HOUSEHOLD ENVIRONMENT

The first and most obvious place to start is your home. I don't think it's going too far to say that our homes, and the way we arrange them, are outward manifestations of our inner lives. And if the vision you have for how you would like your home to look and feel is different from how it actually looks and feels, then you have more than just tidying and decorating to do. You need to do some inner work too.

Imagine for a second that your home has a personality and is another member of your family. Now let's say that your home supports you in the best way it possibly can. What do you think it would be like?

My vision is that my home would be able to breathe. Belongings would each have their own space, and the floors and surfaces would be clear when not in use. We would be able to move through the rooms and locate and use items with ease. The house would not be burdened with unloved and redundant objects. It would be decorated in a way that brings me happiness. It would be alert at all times, equally ready to provide space for daily tasks, and also to receive visitors. My house would be set up to support us inhabitants in the activities and routines that we do *now*, not those we did three years ago, or aspire to do in the future.

My house would be warm, secure and familiar. I would understand and appreciate its features and qualities, its quirks and idiosyncrasies. The fabric of the house would be well maintained, without grumbling, and regular, loving cleaning would make it a pleasant and healthy place to be, for even the most ordinary tasks. My house would nurture my family and me, and make living in it a joy.

I'm not there yet. But this is where I hope to live someday.

I think that the work of clearing and maintaining our homes is intrinsically linked to the work of clearing and maintaining our minds. In both tasks we need to be persistent in establishing and reinforcing healthy, daily habits. This means coming back to the breath whenever we remember. Putting away the craft stuff when we have finished with it or washing a plate rather than leaving it on the table. And we also need to do a fair bit of clearing out. It's easy to see how to do this in our house. We just need to give away unwanted clutter. For our minds the task is subtler, but

I get the feeling it's about letting go of the unhelpful beliefs and assumptions that we have built up over a lifetime. 'I'm terrible with money.' 'I have a quick temper.' 'I can't possibly get this house tidy because my husband is so disorganized.' These are the modes of thinking that hold us back and stop us from reaching our potential as human beings.

Now I need to hold my hand up right away and say that I am an extremely untidy person. My friends and family will find it hilarious that I am trying to give advice about tidiness. I have spent much of my life trying to find ways to store and organize my mountains of belongings, only to find myself living in a sea of mess again the following day. As a child I remember pulling drawing pins out of my heel, because I hadn't seen a spilt box among all the debris on my floor. More recently, tidying up for a social occasion is a major operation normally requiring two or three days of solid work, and often involving one or more bedrooms becoming out of bounds to guests, as it becomes the dumping ground for all the belongings with no home.

It was shortly after our second child was born that I realized I had to do something about it. I was sitting on the sofa breastfeeding him surrounded by disorder. I couldn't bear it any longer. So I started to research how to be tidy. I followed housekeeping websites and bought Shelia Chandra's wonderful book *Banish Clutter Forever*.[13] And I came to understand that I habitually commit the two great sins of untidiness – being both a hoarder and failing to complete tasks. I hate waste, so I can't walk past a skip without peering in to see if there is anything I want. But the irony is that I often have to buy multiple tools and resources, because I can't find the originals amidst the clutter. And things get broken, or mouldy, as they languish in piles in corners. I acquire too much stuff, I hang onto it for too long, and I don't put things away when I've finished with them. To make matters worse my husband is the same.

I realized that we simply had far too much stuff and, although we were afraid to let things go, the stuff we were holding on to was making us unhappy. To make things more complicated, we were also going through a period of major building work, so we also had to contend with masses of equipment and materials. In between breastfeeds, I went on a mission to clear our house. We sent literally vanloads of stuff to the tip, and around 30 sacks to the charity shop.

Four years later, we are still working on it but we have made massive progress. DIY projects cause temporary setbacks, but in general the trend is toward more order and beauty. A renewed effort this last month has seen us able to clear a further 15 sacks to the charity shop – 10 of these from our bedroom, the room where I meditate. Simply sitting in a clear space becomes a pleasure.

CHILDREN GENERATE STUFF

Now, even if you were a reasonably tidy and organized person before you had children, you probably still had a house full of belongings. But I can safely predict that since having a child or two, you have become inundated with equipment, toys and clothes. You spend weekends buying new toy chests, books cases and under-bed storage containers. A lot of people try to solve this problem by buying a bigger house. But even then the stuff just keeps on coming.

SO WHAT'S THE PROBLEM WITH STUFF?

The problem with stuff is that most of it is surplus to requirements. And possessions seem to have a life force of their own. They are often physical manifestations of unmade decisions and failed intentions. Even if they are out of sight, they still weigh on our minds. Take my bread maker, for example. I had very good intentions of waking up to fresh bread baking each morning. And I actually did it for a week or two. But I really hated the way the paddle got stuck in the bottom of the loaf. I put it away in the cupboard, thinking I'd get it out again once our new kitchen was finished. It languished there and I felt slightly guilty every time I had to shove it to one side to drag the vacuum cleaner past (which admittedly, wasn't very often).

And then there are the piles and piles of paperwork that I keep meaning to sort through, but never do. It weighs on my mind, creating an underlying feeling of anxiety. And because it gets in such a mess, important jobs and documents sometimes get lost or forgotten, causing moments of acute stress. Like when we were about to go on holiday to France, and I couldn't find my daughter's passport.

It's not easy to stay mindful in these conditions. Our belongings tug at our attention, reminding us of the sewing project we never got round to finishing. Or there are simply so many of them that they become a barrage of debris, confusing and hindering us at every turn. They become a sort of physical 'to do' list – one that we literally trip over as we try to go about our business.

BE HONEST ABOUT HOW YOU WOULD LIKE YOUR HOME TO BE

Now I'm not saying that your home needs to be pristine, with minimalist design and décor. Being too rigid with tidiness and cleanliness can be equally unhelpful. It may inhibit creativity and playfulness in both yourself and your children. I've noticed that children from very tidy homes can find our house and garden really liberating, as they delight in finding bits of old flower pots and pieces of wood and such like floating around the garden and using them as props in their play. They like the fact that they can help themselves to paint and it doesn't matter if it gets on the grass – or even inside on the tiles. The trick is to try to visualize what a beautiful, helpful home would look like for *your family*. Just as I said before with routines (in Chapter 4, see page 35), make sure that your house serves *your* needs, rather than you tiptoeing around the 'needs' of your house.

THE EFFECT OF BELONGINGS ON OUR CHILDREN

I've talked a lot about how belongings can impact on our own inner worlds, but they affect our children too. Just like us, shelves crammed with books and knick-knacks will stimulate our children. But while having a certain amount is important, it's very easy to have too much. It turns into a kind of background noise that we become adept at tuning out. But how refreshing when the sound is actually turned off! Overfull drawers and cupboards will make it much harder for children to find and use equipment by themselves, in their path toward independence.

But the real influence comes from those objects that are specifically designed to be of interest to children, namely: toys.

WE DON'T NEED TOYS FOR PLAY

I've had the occasional conversation when I have complained about the number of toys in our house and admitted I'd like to chuck them all out. 'But you know it's really important for children to play?' has come the slightly shocked response. Of course it's important for children to play. Play is fundamental to the development and wellbeing of our children. Toys, however, are not. Yet somehow (and it's probably a lot of advertising that is responsible for this), we have come to equate toys with play.

HOW MANY TOYS DO YOU NEED?

Kim John Payne writes about the power of less in his book *Simplicity Parenting*.[14] He argues that by decreasing the quantity of children's toys, we can enable them to play more deeply with the ones that they have. Let's imagine a child playing in the dirt outside a mud hut in Africa. How many toys do you think he has? Perhaps one or two?

How many toys does your child(ren) have? Ten, twenty? Fifty ... a hundred? ... *a thousand*? If you only have one baby it's possible that you do only have a handful of toys – especially if you are yet to pass a birthday or Christmas. But left unchecked, by the time they are preschoolers or older, children can own an extraordinary amount of toys – even if you don't count the Lego individually. Now the main issue I have with the sheer quantity of toys is that they so easily end up spewed across the floor, which makes it difficult for me to enjoy living in my house. I've seen the same effect on my children. They love walking into their room after it's been tidied. The freshly hoovered rug invites them to sit and engage more deeply and calmly, whereas a carpet strewn with tiny bits and bobs is not even seen as a play space.

Payne says that play is equivalent to a kind of meditation for children.[15] I think this is a really interesting idea. I don't think it's completely obvious how meditation works for children, and I'll be discussing this in more depth in Chapter 11. But it is certainly true that deep, uninterrupted play enables creativity and leaves children calm and satisfied.

Too many toys – especially when they are on view at all times – create a very distracting environment and makes concentration harder. Any parent who has survived at least one Christmas will recognize how frazzled children get when they are bombarded with too many presents. Birthdays and festivals are extreme examples, but when we allow our children to have free access to an abundance of toys then we are willingly making this kind of excess our everyday reality.

I think that demonstrating mindful enjoyment of simple things ourselves, like getting outside or doing craft activities, is more effective than trying to rationally argue against consumerism.

Ed, dad to Ruth, 9

TYPES OF TOYS

Have a think about the nature of a toy. It's designed to stimulate and capture the attention. Toy companies want it to be a success as soon as it is unwrapped and out of the box. In order to get the biggest impact, toys tend to be brightly coloured with flashing lights and noisy sounds. Relatives love giving these sorts of gifts to their younger family members. Imagine living in a room surrounded by these alarming objects. In fact – you probably don't even need to imagine it – because for many of us this is our life. If a toy is annoying and grating to you, it almost certainly is equally or more stimulating to your child. In order to cope with living in such an environment they presumably have to learn to 'tune out' the background noise. This is the opposite of mindfulness.

I tend to think of toys – especially flashy ones – like recreational drugs for children. I've known parents to say, 'Well, we used to get wooden ones at first, but then his Auntie got him that flashing Bob the Builder over there and he just loves it. So we got him the whole set.' Of course he loves it! Toys like this are designed to give instant gratification. A quick fix of excitement. Of course they'll go for this one over the old wooden one that 'doesn't do anything.' But the point is, they'll play with it differently too. Instead of engaging with it and imagining a character or a scenario, or a way that it can interact with the other toys or the furniture, the flashing Bob the Builder comes with its own character and script.

I'm not being totally fair. I've seen plenty of children play imaginatively with such toys. And sometimes a particular character can give them a nudge toward play in a whole new area. But it may be harder for them to be creative. Occasionally you will find onlookers – adults and children, maybe even yourself – helping the child to 'play with it properly' (i.e. the way the manufacturer has designed). And it's certainly harder for them to go back to the 'boring' toys afterward, especially if they are sitting alongside the exciting ones in the toy box. When my son was about 18 months old, and he was sitting in his high chair waiting for dinner, if he didn't have any toy he used to pretend that his hands were cars, and play with those instead. Nowadays it's much harder for him to make do with the simpler toys. Our children are learning to rely on outside stimulants to keep them entertained, instead of the resources of their own minds.

PRUNING THE TOY PILE

So my advice is that you should take stock of the number and kinds of toys you provide for your child. Ask yourself, are these *really* the kinds of toys you want your child playing with? And how many toys can your child value? Keep only a few toys on display and store some quality ones for rotation. Chuck out the rest. Payne suggests doing this without the input of your children. I disagree with him on this. I think it's worth helping your children learn how to let go of toys as soon as possible. Also, depending on their age, they may feel really betrayed if you discard something that they value. Because this is related to cultivating generosity, I discuss how to go about this in depth in Chapter 10.

Most likely it will be your relatives who will be the biggest obstacle to keeping the toys under control. They mean well, but the older generation especially have grown up in a different era when presents and treats were scarcer. They delight in giving generously to their grandchildren – and hey, what's wrong with that? It's lovely that they care. But we still need to be careful about the accumulation of toys – which is something that gets forgotten when the grandparent or auntie is wrapping up the gift. In previous years, I've given guidance to our extended family about the types of toys we do and don't want. Sometimes they politely ignore me, but most often they ask me in advance what the children would like. I have been known to insist that certain presents be kept for play at Grandma's house. Where possible I try to steer both children and gift-givers in the direction of experiences, such as tickets to the pantomime, or a rock-climbing course.

SIMPLIFYING THEIR TIMETABLE

Just as we need to protect our children's need for a simplified environment in which to play, we also need to be aware of allowing them enough *time* to play – so they can become naturally absorbed in the task at hand. In our desire to offer opportunities for our children, there can be a temptation to enrol them into countless classes and activities.

Now I'm not denying the benefit of these classes. Because of the constrained nature of life in the West, where work, social and family arenas tend to be strictly segregated, I think it is important that we consciously expose our children to various activities. For example, our children may not have access to much dance, singing or music within the home environment; in contrast, a child from a tribal society may have this daily. Another example might be swimming – children may only be able to learn if they attend scheduled classes, or at least open sessions during the pool's opening hours. But I think it's really important that we also consider how much time our children have for uninterrupted, child-led play. Because they need a lot of this.

It's not just the children who need more time. We parents also need to take a step back from our timetables and check that we haven't taken on too many responsibilities and commitments. Although it might seem as if cramming as much into the day as possible leads to a fuller life, in fact, when we are rushing from one job or activity to another, it can become very difficult to really appreciate *any* of the activities that we do.

But don't get caught in the trap of thinking – oh I'm too busy to be mindful. We can still raise mindfulness when we are rushing around. However, it's important to be realistic about how your schedule interacts with your mental state – just as the orderliness (or chaos) of your house feeds into your mind too. When we have too many jobs to do, we are constantly going over all the little thoughts associated with tasks, trying not to forget anything. This is stressful, and not conducive to calm and mindfulness. And when we do inevitably forget something, or arrive late, or forget to put the washing machine on, simply because there wasn't enough time, then this causes knock-on negative consequences and associated negative thoughts.

When you have a new baby, your day can slow down almost to a halt. But once the children are a little older, their clubs and activities can take over. The trick is to try to strike a balance. Perhaps take a step back and work out where you might be able to simplify and make time for more calm. This is just as, if not *more*, important than all the other activities. You can earmark time for you and your child to be together, just doing whatever type of play or activity they would like to do – baking a cake, going to the park or building Lego. You can use this time for mindful connection with your child, giving both of you a chance to replenish and to strengthen your relationship.

When I'm busy and overly committed, I notice that I have a tendency to resist my children's calls for my attention. 'Not now,' or 'OK, but only for five minutes.' When my mind is reaching toward the end of the activity, instead of being mindfully engaged in my son's game, I can find the play irksome. Through mindfulness I can notice my resistance to fully playing and then I can make a choice. I can either decide to stop playing – perhaps by negotiating a rest – or I can simply observe my resistance and watch it rise and fall. Because it will pass! (Although that sometimes feels hard to believe.) And when it does, and we reach a deeper level of commitment to the task at hand, it magically becomes more interesting.

Of course, what sometimes happens is that instead of observing my feelings without judgement, I unconsciously act them out – perhaps tensing up, or looking at the clock. I remind my son that it's just two more minutes left of bath time and use my body in a limited way, as if I feel I have to conserve as much energy as possible. The problem with this (and we all do it from time to time) is that your child will almost certainly intuitively pick up on your lack of engagement. When we play begrudgingly,

---

TIP: Planning

Practical ways to assess your week:

- Write out a weekly planner for each person in your house.
- Consider how much time you and your children spend outside, especially in free play.
- Consider where you can slow down the pace. Can you allow a few extra minutes for the school run, to allow time to look down drains?
- Have you built in time for being together – no specific activity, just being?

---

it sends a confusing message about self-respect. Our negative feeling can become the white elephant in the room that your child senses but doesn't know how to name. This kind of halfway house of dragging our feet can make everyone feel unsatisfied. I've noticed that when I play like this, my son gets increasingly annoyed with me, and becomes even more bossy and needy – which creates a vicious cycle of me finding the game even more irksome, until eventually I am pushed to the point of refusing to play any more.

In an ideal world, we either agree to do something and then do it wholeheartedly, or we say no. In this respect, we can learn a lot from our children. For young children, it seems almost impossible to get them to do a task unwillingly. If you have ever tried to get a toddler to walk when they are tired, you'll know what I mean. That's why it is so helpful to be creative and playful when we are trying to win children over to a certain task, such as brushing their teeth, or putting them in the car seat. But once they are engaged, they absolutely throw themselves into it.

As children get older, their minds start to skip ahead to plans or back over past events, just as we adults do. That's a natural part of growing up. But we can do a lot to protect time, both theirs and ours, so that a frantic mind doesn't become a necessary strategy for coping with an overloaded world.

SCREEN TIME

Research tells us that too much TV interferes with brain development. It can reduce IQ, increase aggression and cause problems with attention. For example, a recent Japanese study showed that the brain structure actually changes depending on how many hours are spent watching TV.[16]

These findings terrify me. Because although I know that TV is potentially damaging, I still let my children watch too much of it. And I'm not alone. Ofcom estimates that 3–4-year-olds spend an average of 3 hours a day in front of a screen; teenagers, 6.5 hours. In the US, the TV is on virtually all the time in 40 per cent of homes.[17]

TV AND MINDFULNESS

I think screen time also has an impact on our ability to raise mindfulness, in both children and adults. When we imagine certain events or scenarios, our bodies respond as if those scenarios are real. So, for example, thinking about something scary can make our hearts beat faster. It is possible to notice this reaction or not, depending on how much mindfulness we have at the time. When we are watching TV, it is as if the TV is 'thinking' for us. This means that our emotions and body are responding to the content of the TV show, as if it were a real situation. We are being taken on a rollercoaster ride without even realizing it.

It can be very hard to remain mindful during a TV programme. Recently my husband and I watched a great film about a man who was paralyzed from the neck down. At the end, my husband commented that it had been really well acted. At that moment, I realized that throughout the film it had never once occurred to me they were acting. Despite the fact that I have a well-established meditation practice, I completely lose myself when watching a film.

The world of the film becomes utterly absorbing and believable for me. This has potential implications if the creators of the film have some kind of political or social message, or perhaps just a limiting worldview. If *I* can't (or don't try to) maintain awareness as I watch, then what chance does a three-year-old have?

One of the problems with watching, as opposed to say, reading, is that we can't regulate the rate at which we are stimulated. When we read a book with a child, there is the opportunity to modify the story, to slow down or to skip over sections, to provide commentary ('That bit was really scary, wasn't it?'). We can use these kinds of interactions to remind our child that we are reading a book, if it seems that we need that little bit of extra distance – or mindfulness. We can't do this with the TV, however: it just keeps on coming.

I'm sure that the content of programmes also plays a part. Fast-paced action stories give us that excitement fix. There is an experiment where monkeys in a cage can press a button to access a small amount of cocaine.[18] They just keep on pressing the button, over and over again. Our children are like that with TV. It's so *easy* to have this intense kind of stimulation. The fact that the programmes aren't ultimately satisfying (other people's triumphs and failures can't keep them interested for long) doesn't stop them reaching for that quick fix. The content also feeds into their worldview. Aggressive behaviour on-screen often equates directly to aggression in our children. (I'll talk more about good guys and bad guys in Chapter 8.) Mindfulness is about noticing and accepting the reality that we are presented with. But our children, especially young ones, can't distinguish between TV and reality. And even when stories have a moral message attached, often that's not the bit that children remember.

TV also indirectly weakens chances for mindfulness by limiting the amount of time left over for play and high-quality social interaction. We've already seen that playtime needs to be protected. TV works rather like a dummy (pacifier), in that it keeps our children occupied so we can effectively switch off from them. This is bad news for our own mindful connection with our children.

After watching television, my son becomes frustrated because he wants to keep watching it. He plays and interacts with us more happily and calmly when other activities come to a close, so I limit television to times when it is helpful. For example, a little TV time can be helpful while I am cooking.

Kate, mum to Zach, 2½

WHY DO WE LET THEM WATCH SO MUCH TV?

For me there are two reasons: one is that it can be really hard to say no, the other is that it's convenient. The TV can keep children occupied and give us parents a break. Last year, when I was struggling with some emotional problems, and at the same time I had taken on far too much work, I realized that some days had passed when my three-year-old had spent virtually all day watching (more on difficult feelings in Chapter 9). A poll suggests 85 per cent of mums admit to using a screen as a babysitter.[19] When you are desperately trying to get the dinner on the table, or you need to make an important phone call, or it's the middle of the night and your child won't go back to sleep, the TV can feel like an absolute miracle worker.

So it's hard for us to enforce limits on TV watching, because it's pretty darn tempting for us parents to let them have a few more minutes.

HOW EFFECTIVE A BABYSITTER IS TV ANYWAY?

Although TV seems to keep our children occupied, in the medium to long term I think it can make life harder for parents. The problem with TV is that our children become dependent on it. Last year, my son used to ask if he could watch TV as soon as he woke up. As soon as children are bored, they instantly think

TIP: Creative ways to reduce screen time

- Check if you are over-relying on the TV as a babysitter. Sometimes this can get out of hand.
- If TV watching is habitual at certain times, change the routine to pre-empt watching.
- Twos and under can normally be distracted away from the TV. It's more difficult when older siblings are around, so pay attention to how and where older children watch.
- Consider how you store and display your screens. If you install your TV prominently on the living room wall, this sends a strong message about how much you value it. Store phones and tablets out of sight when they are not being used.
- Disable the watching and games functions on your phone.
- Tell your child why it's worrying, in a way they can understand. 'The doctor said that children need lots of time for playing so their brains work properly. If you watch too much television, there won't be enough time to play.'
- Suggest they come up with their own ways to reduce screen time. This might be limiting the number of programmes watched, only watching their favourite show, or only allowing TV up to, or after a certain time of day. It will be easier to hold them to their own plan.
- Agree on an interesting activity that you can do instead of watching the television such as baking, play-dough or craft.
- Many children go to the TV to get their story fix. Pre-empt with lots of reading.
- Work out a list of activities that need to be ticked off each day before watching TV can take place, e.g. tidy the bedroom, play outside, read a book, sing a song, make something crafty. They may get so involved with one of these activities that they forget about the TV.

of the TV. Watching becomes their default mode. This means that they continually look to an outside source for stimulation. It also means that children don't learn how boredom passes into creativity. And this isn't just a long-term effect: we can see it happening just over the course of a day. After a couple of hours of watching TV, children are listless and irritable. They lose the ability to be self-resourceful. If they are suddenly without a screen, perhaps because you have imposed a limit, they can seem very needy for your attention. And you probably have lots of things to do! This becomes a vicious circle, making it even more difficult to take the TV away.

The good news is that although children find it very difficult to regulate screen time, they learn habits extremely easily. It only takes a day or so without the TV for children to relearn how to engage in self-directed play. So before long, you'll be able to do the dishes as your three-year-old organizes the animals into a parade, with only the occasional input as competition judge.

AVOIDING SHOPS

When babies and toddlers are still able to ride in a sling or sit contentedly in a buggy, then going round the shops can seem like a non-event. However, once children start getting more alert to their environment, and a clearer sense of what they want to do, then going shopping can quickly turn into a nightmare of tantrums, tumbling packets and dirty looks at the checkout queue.

Young children can get absolutely overwhelmed by the sheer amount of interesting stuff that is on display in a supermarket. Take a moment to look at the shop through your child's eyes: row upon row of brightly coloured packaging and interesting items, all in grabbing distance. This kind of stimulation can get very tiring, especially when combined with continual instructions, 'Don't touch!' 'Put that back!' The hour-and-a-half-long supermarket trip can seem to be interminable.

My answer to this is: avoid, avoid, avoid. Actually, with a bit of tweaking of your weekly routine, avoiding shops becomes rather easy. Instead of a weekly supermarket visit, you can buy online and have your groceries home delivered. We have our milk delivered and also a fruit and veg box. I don't even have to order them online, as I have set up a standard delivery. This takes a lot of the hassle out of shopping for us adults too. By forgoing the weekly supermarket shop, it does mean that we end up popping to our local shop on a more regular basis, but somehow this seems easier to manage. And, as it only takes 10 minutes, it can easily be done once the children are in bed.

Avoiding shops altogether also has the advantage that both you and your children are less exposed to advertising, which has a habit of creeping into every public space. Like toys and TV, adverts are designed to be eye-catching and stimulating. We are constantly having our attention diverted to the next product. It's very hard to remain mindful under such conditions, and easy to get overwhelmed, for both adults and children.

TIP: Keeping shopping fun

If you do have to go to the shops together, then you can reduce the sensory overload by slowing down the task, perhaps by taking time to mindfully explore the fruit and veg aisle – noting all the different smells and textures and colours.

BEING IN NATURE

In Chapter 5, I discussed how we need to make time for opportunities to reconnect, especially as our children grow older and play more independently (see page 63). This can be surprisingly hard. Even when I have decided that I will really join my child in play, somehow I still end up doing a chore within the space of about five minutes ('I'll just quickly hang the washing out, and then we can play some more.') What happens in these scenarios is that after a short period of play, some kind of irritation or boredom surfaces. Instead of mindfully noting that feeling and letting it rise and fall away, I look for a way to relieve it. I scan through my mental 'to do' list and convince myself that the next job on it must be done right now.

The problem with this is that we may well leave our child feeling short-changed. Especially if this is something we have a habit of doing often. And it doesn't really help us either. Because *really* mindful play with our child – the type of place we get to when we make the effort to stick it through the boring bits – can do a huge amount to replenish ourselves. Afterward we feel good about ourselves, proud that we have re-established the connection with our child. And proud that we completed the task we undertook to do.

Losing our attention and flitting on to another job partway into some activity with our child can actually leave us feeling unsatisfied and restless. One way to combat this is to set up an activity that requires a higher level of commitment. I find that a really great way to commit to some mindful play with my children is to go outside with them. Ideally somewhere further afield than the garden. Although I can't guarantee that this will lead to a high-quality experience between us, at least I am setting myself up with the right conditions. When we are out at the park, or walking in the woods, I have put myself in a position where I can't be distracted by the laundry or my emails. (Luckily my phone has some mobile data issue that I am not in a hurry to fix.) It's much easier for me to immerse myself in the moment, and to share in my child's world.

NATURE WITHOUT EGO

But it's not just about removing the distractions of the home. Being in nature is also conducive to mindfulness in its own right. The sights, sounds and smells of nature seem to have a quality that is both at once rich and yet also not overstimulating.

I think there is something incredibly soothing about the experience of being surrounded by such harmony. There is no ego in nature. Each animal, plant, rock, drop of water, goes about its business without any agenda. The brown leaves do not complain when autumn comes and it is their turn to be nudged from the twigs of the tree. Every single thing that we see is setting an example to us – teaching us how to allow the world to be as it is.

Of course, we could argue that objects that are connected with human activity – such as computers, traffic lights, cars – must also inherently follow the laws of nature. But it is much harder to see the simplicity of these artefacts and machines, when so many egos have been involved in their making. So being outdoors in nature is both a literal and metaphorical blast of fresh air. It gives us a chance to have a break from the way we respond to all these complicated human-made objects, which have often been designed to elicit some kind of response from us. Being in nature drastically reduces the number of stimulants we are being bombarded with, and gives us a chance to choose consciously where we place our attention. This is true for both children and adults. That's why making the effort to spend time outside in nature always seems to pay off.

SUMMARY

- *Your home environment both reflects and influences your inner world. Clutter can become a physical 'to-do' list of unmade decisions. It can hinder and limit you, making mindfulness harder. Overhauling your home can go hand-in-hand with maintaining you mind.*
- *Toys are designed to stimulate. Too many can actually obstruct your child's deep play. Choose toys wisely and keep the quantity under control.*
- *Beware of overscheduling. Children need time as well as space to engage in deep play. You need breathing time too.*

- *Too much screen time can reduce the time for free play, and undermine children's ability to play creatively. It can limit their ability to be self-resourceful and mindful.*
- *Spend some time in nature. Nature provides a rich environment without being over-stimulating. It frees us from screens and advertising, and allows us the perfect conditions to reconnect.*

7

Mindful Speaking and Listening

The way we speak and listen is so important to our relationships that I think it is worth devoting a whole chapter to this subject. Of course, we communicate by other means too. Our body language, facial expressions and our actions also convey a great deal. But given that we think in words, and place such a great emphasis on them, speech is the obvious place to start. When we start to make conscious decisions about the way we speak, this impacts on our communication as a whole.

THE INCESSANT VOICE

Almost everybody has a voice inside their head that talks incessantly. For many people, this voice sounds exactly like their own voice. Right now, my voice is dictating the words I should be typing for this chapter. Sometimes the voice serves a useful function; at other times it provides unhelpful and unasked for advice. We can often find our voices commenting on the past or present, or having imagined conversations in the future.

We have a tendency to identify very strongly with this voice. Before I started practising mindfulness, I didn't even realize I had a voice. *I thought that voice was me.* Being able to see (at least at times) that the voice inside my head is not, in fact, me is one of the *major* benefits of mindfulness. Sometimes, my voice will dictate a sentence that's concise and pertinent; at other times, my voice will ramble on or go down a dead end. Sometimes it might suggest something to write that sounds downright odd.

Luckily, I don't have to obey my voice, because there is some part of me that remains an observer, which can discern whether I've composed a good sentence or not, and choose whether to develop it or scrap it. As the observer, I don't need to have a big mental discussion to make a decision. I can simply sense whether the words are right for now. I'll look back at the text later, make more edits, and eventually a team of editors and proofreaders will comb through it too.

Now the same principle can be applied with speaking. Sometimes, when we are faced with a situation, our voice will come up with a comment. Often we'll simply start articulating the words, without even making a decision to talk. The problem with this is that sometimes (just like with my writing) the voice comes up with some really duff things to say. But unfortunately with speaking, once the words are out there, there's nothing you can do to take them back. You won't get a copy-editor checking if you really meant that. So, with speaking, it pays to be really careful – that is, mindful – as we choose our words.

Usually the most mindful thing to do in heated situations
is not to talk at all, just to listen and then give the other
person a lot of space, whether that's my wife or my son.
But it's a very difficult practice.
Ben, dad to Leo, 6

BREAKING FREE OF SCRIPTS

Where do these ill-judged comments come from? Very often the voice inside our head simply parrots scripts it has heard before. When a situation triggers some kind of negative memory or feeling from the past, your mind comes up with some pithy comment to accompany it. It might be something you heard your parents say when you were a child, or it might be something you read in the newspaper or heard on the bus last week. The voice itself may even turn into the voice of an authority figure from your past. It might not be exactly the same words – sometimes we just soak up a certain tone or inflection, which later infects the way we speak.

Whenever I feel under pressure, or cling to a need for control, then the tendency is to revert to script, which tends to set up a negative spiral, until mindfulness reminds me that I have the option to step back from the low-budget soap opera that I've created!

Gwil, meditation teacher and dad to a son, 6, and daughter, 3

I'll give you an example. Not long after I began childminding, and once I had started meditating, I started picking up a five-year-old from school. As this girl was three years older than my eldest, some of her behaviour was new to me. One day, during a break on the way home, she took a snack from her bag. When she had opened it, I watched her casually drop the wrapper on the ground. I could feel anger welling up inside me – I have always hated littering. The voice inside my head started to react. But because I had learnt to call up some mindfulness, I listened to the words instead of voicing them directly: *If you don't pick up that wrapper immediately, you won't get any dinner when you get home.* The harsh-sounding words themselves made me feel even angrier. I could almost see the authority figures from my past nodding in approval. So I took another breath to let the feeling subside a little. This pause helped me remember that a) I was her childminder and I had a duty to provide her with dinner (so that threat was completely ridiculous), and b) she's just a five-year-old, and obviously hasn't yet learnt the significance of littering.

With another breath I saw that a much more helpful response would be to help her learn that littering was undesirable. I could do that gently and without shaming her. Feeling much calmer, I picked up the wrapper and silently put it in a nearby bin.

I saw that she had observed me do it, and we went on our way back home.

I remember asking my meditation teacher at the time whether I was doomed to hear these scripts forever. He explained to me that as mindfulness becomes more developed, and we get better at recognizing what's happening in our minds, eventually, we may be able to spot the anger arising before it 'presses play' on the voiceover. So we can intercept the process before the voice even starts talking. Over the years since I started meditating, I have found that to be the case more and more. But still sometimes I am surprised at the harsh, vicious or vindictive voice that sometimes starts talking in my head, and I am shocked that I am even imagining saying those things to my precious children.

When I'm feeling well, have had enough sleep and am not under pressure, it's easy to have mindful speech. Put simply you 'think before you speak'. Sometimes if something comes out that's not quite right I'm immediately aware of it, almost a physical sensation in my gut or chest that I said something unskilful.

Jan, mum to Josia, 8 and Hannah, 5

SPEAKING GENTLY

So what sort of language do we want to use toward our children? Because we are so close to our children, and they know how to push our buttons, it is often easy to disregard the common rules of courtesy and kindness when we talk to them. We may find ourselves nagging or shouting at them, or even casually shaming or berating them. Most of the time we don't even know we are doing it.

- 'Can't you keep your knife on the table?'
- 'Get into the car seat RIGHT NOW.'

- 'Don't be so disgusting.'
- 'I've had enough of you.'

However, when we hear other parents talk like this to their children, our ears prick up, and we may wince at the negativity that's being passed back and forth. When we have a bit of perspective, we know that these harsh ways of talking don't make us, or our children, feel happier. They make us all feel worse. And much of the time, the words are not even effective in the short term. Instead of putting her coat on, your toddler may start crying. A tantruming two-year-old may simply scream harder at being told to 'shut up'. This type of language, when repeated time and time again may also have unintended consequences in the long term. Children grow into adults believing that they are not quite good enough, or that they should be ashamed of themselves, and as parents they are predisposed to repeat these same old scripts again.

USING MINDFULNESS TO CHOOSE OUR WORDS

So how do we know what kind of speech is helpful, and what is unhelpful? Various cultures have come up with guidelines for helpful speech. Victorian moralists came up with the three criteria to ask of oneself: is it *true*, *kind* and *necessary*? Buddhism adds *timely* to this list. I'll discuss these factors in a little more depth later on in this chapter.

But of course there are no instructions as to which specific sentences are correct and which are not. It all depends on the particular circumstances, the background and the individuals involved. As parents, *you* know your child best. I can't tell you how you should speak to him or her. But what I *do* know is that very often, parents don't use their own knowledge of their children and the circumstances when they speak to them. Instead of assessing the situation coolly, when we are triggered we react with whatever comes into our heads, knee-jerk style.

Bringing mindfulness to our speech by shining a torch on it can help us begin to speak in a way that reflects our aspiration to be

TIP: Strategies to raise mindfulness

When you find yourself in a potentially stressful situation, these tricks may help you stay mindful and prevent you saying things that will make the situation worse or that you later regret.

Pretend you are on CCTV, and you'll get the opportunity to watch the film later. Are you speaking in a way you'll be embarrassed about? Or will you sound OK? Just momentarily bringing to mind the video camera, can help to gain a bit of perspective. (Once, when my daughter was having a tantrum, I actually did video us. I had the idea that I might show some sympathetic person at a later date what a hard time I'd had. Having the camera recording made me determined to behave impeccably – I was at my most understanding and reasonable!)

A similar trick is to imagine that someone you really respect is listening to you. Choose someone who understands what you are aiming for, not someone who would judge you by your children's behaviour. Sometimes the thought of a person can bring out the best in us. That might be a beloved family member, a teacher or a good friend.

A twist on this is to fleetingly imagine that your child actually *is* that someone that you really respect. Ask yourself, 'Would I say this to Great Gran, or my boss?' Just try to conjure up the attitude that you would have while speaking to that other person, and talk to your child in the same spirit.

One that I find works for me is to remember that I am modelling speech. I am not only communicating, but also teaching. Children invariably imitate the way we talk – whether they are talking back to us, or to their peers or siblings. When you are about to say something, ask yourself if you are happy for your children to speak these words/use this tone. It is so incredibly gratifying when we hear our well-chosen words coming out of *their* mouths at a later date.

good parents. We all have good intentions and mindfulness can help us be the parents we want to be. And of course that's going to be beneficial to our children, but perhaps more importantly, it's going to be beneficial to us too. Feeling proud of the way we have spoken, feeling that we have done a good job, especially in a challenging situation, can be very empowering. Or it may be more important to recognize the value in biting our tongues and not saying something hurtful. Refraining from lashing out can be hard work. Yet the value of *not* doing something harmful is not often recognized. We won't get a certificate, but actually it's even more important and far-reaching. Imagine a world where no one said anything harmful.

Speaking mindfully may seem like a lot to remember. But actually, with practice, it starts to feel very natural, until it is our default mode of communicating. Speaking itself becomes a 'mindfulness activity', in the same way that we might specifically practise mindfulness while washing the dishes or walking up the stairs (see page 22). During particularly mindful periods, every conversation that we have with our child is an opportunity for joyful connection.

YOUR PARTNER AS A LIGHTNING ROD

Sometimes we can put a lot of effort into the way we talk to our children, but we neglect to extend the same effort to our partners. They can become an unknowing lightning rod, unexpectedly taking the full force of our rage.

THINKING OUR PARTNERS SHOULD BEHAVE BETTER

It's not surprising we sometimes feel our partners should know how to behave. They are grown up, after all. But when we fall into the trap of expecting them to behave in a certain way, then we are not really allowing the situation to be as it is. We are not acknowledging that circumstances have led to this exact situation. Reacting by getting angry and speaking harshly is a type of resistance. With more mindfulness, we can start to recognize when we are denying the reality of the situation, and instead start to think how our speech can be used to better effect.

FORGETTING TO SHOW CONSIDERATION TO OUR PARTNERS

Now I'm sure that when we really think about it, we know that all people deserve the same respect and courtesy. However, it is easy to get so wrapped up in our children's needs that we start to neglect the needs of others. We start to forget that our partners, too, can be sensitive to the way we speak to them, even if they react in a different way. They are unlikely to burst into tears if we speak harshly to them, but all the same, careless speech will still have an impact and serve to drive us further apart.

FEELING EXHAUSTED

Raising children is hard work, and we need to use a lot of resources to stay patient and loving. More mindfulness makes this process easier, allowing us to draw deeper and deeper from our resources (which are in fact limitless). But there will inevitably be times when mindfulness drops. We may remember not to snap or outwardly display anger, but inwardly we are having a hard time. Living this kind of double life can be utterly exhausting. We may feel so depleted by our interactions with our children that we don't have anything left for our partner. Or we let down our guard in the presence of our partner, and all the tensions come out. This situation is so sad because ironically we are attacking the person who is best placed to support us. There is no quick solution to this scenario – but becoming aware of what's happening can do a lot to help alleviate it.

MAKING A COMMITMENT TO SPEAK KINDLY

This technique is so simple, but so easily overlooked. We can drastically improve the quality of talk between the adults in the house, simply by deciding to speak more kindly. But the important thing here is: don't wait for your partner to start doing this first! Just go right ahead and start speaking kindly to your partner. Even if they are speaking unhelpfully to you or doing things that provoke you, try to use the same criteria for mindful speaking that you use when you talk to your children. The wonderful thing about this strategy is that your partner will respond in kind, making the task increasingly easier, and the habit will soon become ingrained.

ENCOURAGING OUR CHILDREN TO BE POLITE

No matter how mindful you are of your own speech, young children are incapable of being mindful of theirs. They do not yet have the mental capacity to bring that kind of awareness to their speech (or indeed anything else). It will come, perhaps a bit faster with a bit of guidance from you (see Chapter 11), and from age three or four you may occasionally notice some considered speech. But don't count on it. For a long time then, the burden is on us parents to do all the work.

However, there are things that we can do to promote kinder speech. I've already mentioned how children learn through imitation. So the more often we speak kindly to our children and in front of them, the more likely they are to absorb and then replicate these modes of speaking.

But we can do much more than this. It's actually very easy to teach children how to speak politely. We just need to capitalize on the way children learn language. Although this is not strictly about mindfulness in itself, I have found that by changing my own attitude toward my children's speech, and at the same time actively promoting better speech from them, leads to far more harmony in the house as a whole, and helps avoid situations that trigger me. Getting the children to talk politely to us can be a source of major aggravation. Now, I said *easy*. I did not say *fast*. Becoming proficient in any aspect of a language is not a quick process. My four-year-old regularly mixes up his past tenses, saying 'winned' for won, and 'goed' for went, etc. It should therefore be of no surprise that he often forgets to ask nicely and say please and thank you. However,

I am confident that in time he will master both these aspects of language without any need for conflict.

Think of how a baby learns his first words. He points to the sky and says, 'bu!' 'Yes, that's a *bird*,' we answer him. In fact over the next few months, almost every time he speaks we will repeat back his words, modelling the correct version if he has got it wrong or said it unclearly. The new speakers quickly learn what we parents are doing: we are acknowledging the meaning of what they are trying to say and correcting them. And they build on this, acquiring more and more words, becoming ever more clear and articulate.

Of course the system has its complexities. Learning pronouns inevitably causes confusion:

> He points, 'Your cup.'
> 'Yes, that's my cup.'
> A flicker of hesitation, 'My cup . . .' as he hands it to you.

Many parents try to avoid pronouns altogether for this reason. ('Give Mummy's cup to Mummy.') But, in fact, if you persevere toddlers are able to work out the rules surprisingly quickly. Especially if your child has an older sister walking around shouting 'That's MINE!' every time he goes near her belongings.

WHY DEMANDS MAKE US SEE RED

The fact is that please and thank you are simply an aspect of language, just like any other, so we can teach it in the same way. But the irony of the matter is that we often make it difficult for children to learn to say please (especially) and thank you. Consider this exchange.

> 'Bowl!' says your toddler.
> 'You want a bowl? Here you go,' you say.

Nowhere in your reply have you modelled the word please. It is only natural that your toddler will develop this sentence into

'Me want bowl!' Even if at first you don't really notice the lack of the 'please', the words do start to jar eventually. Sometimes it is other people (perhaps family members) who bristle upon hearing a young child ask like this. They may think that the child is being rude or even naughty, and tell them off ('don't you ask like that!').

When impoliteness crops up at the end of a long day, when we have a hundred other jobs to do, being spoken to like this can send us into a spasm of rage. *She's like a little empress and I'm her slave*, we inwardly tell ourselves, all mindfulness out the window. *No wonder my in-laws think she is spoilt.* The fact is that 'please' and 'thank you' are very important words in our culture, and their omission can really rub us up the wrong way. It comes across as ultra-rude. The fact that the children are perilously unaware of the thin ice they have just stepped onto hardly seems to make a difference. If we haven't thought it through in advance it can be so easy to play out the old script and say through gritted teeth, 'Say PLEASE.'

But do we really want them to say *PLEASE* like that? As if it is an accusation? No, of course we don't. And do we want it just to come on its own, as if it's a kind of currency that we will exchange for a bowl? No. We want them to say it lightly and pleasantly, as much a part of the request as all the other words in the sentence.

So why don't they say 'please'? I have heard more sympathetic parents explain it by saying it's a matter of social development, that it's not yet important for them to be polite. Some people argue that new speakers like to be as brief as possible, and so won't use unnecessary words, but I think these ideas overlook the fact that children delight in language and, once they are past the first few months of talking, will often make sentences far more complex than they need to be. I think the matter can be seen in a much simpler light – it's simply a language issue that they haven't yet been taught or acquired fully.

TIP: Teaching polite requests

When your child climbs onto his high chair and says, 'I want bowl.' You can simply confirm you have understood his meaning and provide him with the correct model (just as you did with the bird, see page 101), 'Please can you get me a bowl?' The important thing is to model the sentence *exactly* how you want to hear it, including the tone. Ideally, he'll repeat it back to you without any prompt. If not, and he is old enough, you can gently ask him to give you the whole sentence again. Practising the whole sentence, rather than just the word 'please', means he is much more likely to include 'please' as part of the request next time.

The thing that I find amazing about this technique, is that not only is it effective for teaching, it also prevents me from slipping into a red rage. Instead of seeing my child as a spoilt brat, I simply note that he needs a little more help learning this important skill. The fact that I have given it some thought helps me to be mindful about it. Instead of inwardly feeling angry, my energy goes into implementing the strategy. And the effort it takes to consider how those words could be spoken pleasantly seems to have a transformative effect on my mental state. It's almost as if he *has* said them in that polite way.

Of course, as children get a little older we don't necessarily have to provide the whole sentence. A gentle reminder may suffice. 'Please could you ask that in a nicer way?' But take care to model the tone. That will help both of you keep the conversation light and non-punitive.

SAYING NO

One of the mums in the family meditation class I help to run recently shared how she felt she was constantly saying 'No' to her two-year-old. Almost every interaction with him was beginning with that word. She noticed it was triggering a lot of frustration for him and was causing unnecessary conflict between them. Whenever she felt the impulse to say 'No' she now tried to pause and see if there might be another way to phrase the instruction.

What she found was that in most cases she was able to rephrase the request into a positive instruction. So, for example, 'No. Don't touch the stove,' became, 'Keep your hands back here, where they are safe.'

At other times, however, pausing made her realize that she was restricting him unnecessarily; there was no real reason why he shouldn't do his planned activity. For example, when he began to pull books down from the shelf, instead of saying no, she joined him in his game, and once they were all down, she encouraged him to make a game of putting them back up again. She realized that saying 'no' had become habitual, and at times it was a vocalization of her own reluctance to get connected with his activity.

By making a conscious effort to watch out for times she was saying no, she was in effect turning the impulse to say 'No' into a 'bell of mindfulness' (see page 23). Every time the word surfaced in her mind, she used it as a reminder to pause and check whether she really wanted to speak in that way to her son.

IS YOUR SPEECH TRUE, KIND, NECESSARY AND TIMELY?

Earlier I mentioned the test one can do to check if speech is helpful: is it true, kind, necessary and timely? I think that these criteria are very interesting to consider with regard to family communication, so I will explore them here.

TELLING THE TRUTH

I'm going to talk more about how a commitment to telling the truth supports our personal mindfulness practice in Chapter 10, where I consider ethics in general. Right here, however, I want to look more closely at how truth-telling and lying might affect our relationships with our children.

Take a minute to consider what effect the following untrue statements might have:

- 'I haven't got enough money to buy that.'
- 'If you don't stop shouting, that policeman will come and put you in prison.'

What effect do these sentences have on parent and child? How would they make each feel? I would suggest that they provoke anxiety or disappointment in the child, and disconnection in the parent. So why do we sometimes do it?

Lying may seem a quick and effective way to achieve desired behaviour, but by saying these things, parents are misrepresenting the world. We are leaving our children with an impression that the world is a less good place than it really is. This isn't a good plan for raising children who are confident enough to deal with the challenges of the world that will inevitably come their way.

I would argue that it impacts negatively on parents too, as lying is also a way for us parents to deny reality. It may seem like too much effort to explain the real reasons for certain behaviour. (Sweets are bad for your health. Excessive buying is against our principles. Your shouting is disturbing other people and is socially unacceptable.) Perhaps we do not have enough confidence in our own authority, or we think that the real reason for our instruction will not carry enough weight with our child. Or perhaps we don't want to admit the truth to ourselves. (I can't be bothered to queue up for that. Your shouting is embarrassing me.)

Although it might take longer to explain that too much talking or shouting is unacceptable in this situation, or that we have a headache, or that the noise is disturbing other people, telling the truth in these circumstances forces us to pay more attention to what we are asking our children to do and why. Instead of rattling off a convenient lie, mindfully assessing the situation, facing the reality, and then explaining that reality to our child is far more empowering to both parent and child. In the long term, both will feel better equipped to deal with the world as it really is.

I think I'm true to a fault, some friends find it odd how
much we talked about death with the girls in the final
stages of my mum's terminal illness. In the end it turned
out to be exactly the right approach. They were prepared
for the day when I had to drop everything and run, and
understood all the tears that followed.

Jan, mum to Josia, 8, and Hannah, 5

STORYTELLING

Some parents worry that telling stories and make-believe is also a
kind of lying. I had a discussion with a group of parents about this
recently, and I was interested to see how torn parents felt. Parents
were particularly worried about whether they should pretend
that Father Christmas exists. Some people felt that this equated
to deception. Others argued that encouraging belief in magic
and using the imagination is an important part of childhood
experience. They felt that qualities of playful imagination and
faith would help them in the future. In the case of Santa Claus,
I don't believe there is a specific right or wrong answer. I believe
that the most important thing to consider is what is our *intention*
when we are discussing the matter with our children.

If we say to our children: 'If you don't share nicely, Father
Christmas won't come,' then clearly this is deception in the same
way as in the previous examples. We are using the lie as a tool to
get our preferred behaviour and are disconnecting ourselves with
reality and our children.

Consider this exchange:

> Child: 'Dad, how does Father Christmas' sleigh fly?'
> Dad: 'The reindeer have been to aeronautical school. They
> have to pass an exam before they get on the team.'
> Child: 'How do you know?'
> Dad: 'I watched a documentary about it.'

It may be that this is a playful exchange where father and son are teasing each other. But if the answer is offered in seriousness, then it could be interpreted as a kind of closing down of a child's natural curiosity – this Dad may feel like the myth of Father Christmas should be preserved for as long as possible at all costs. I would argue that in that case, the father is not being truly mindful of his son's needs *at that moment*. His idea of childhood has got in the way of where his son is right now. It may also be that there is a kind of one-upmanship going on here. The Dad is trying to score points for effectively deceiving his son. In order to feel empowered, children need to be able to choose when to acquire or let go of beliefs by themselves. One mum told me how devastated she had been as a child when her friend 'ruined' the Christmas myth for her by telling her the truth.

It's our job as parents to support children in the stage they are currently at – whether that's a playful fantasy world where magic exists, or a curiosity about how the world works on a scientific level. Later it may be even deeper – on a level of spiritual or philosophical enquiry.

When my daughter picked up the idea of Father Christmas from popular culture, I decided not to undeceive her, though also I held back from telling a direct lie. When she asked questions about the mechanics of Christmas, I would answer in this sort of way: 'Some people say that he rides a sleigh pulled by reindeers. In storybooks they say he comes down the chimney. Do you think that's true? How do you think he does it?'

What I liked about this approach was that it invited her to think creatively about the concept and to work out ways to believe or disbelieve, according to her knowledge of the world. Also, it allowed us to guess and fantasize together – it became a shared experience. I even began to wonder myself, on a deeply philosophical level, whether I really did have all the answers. By the time she was five-and-a-half, I felt pretty sure that she knew on one level that it was make-believe, but on another level she was happy to make a conscious choice to believe. In a similar way she has continued to assert that her stuffed animals are alive (and so should never be held by the head).

I think that if we want to encourage our children's imagination, and at the same time give them an opportunity to put their faith in something, then we really need to allow them the opportunity to make choices about their beliefs for themselves. Neither faith nor imagination are engaged if Christmas magic (or indeed any magic) is presented to them as fact. The very nature of magic is that it is something we *can't* explain. If we *know* it to be real, then we can't *believe* in it.

The make-believe figures have become well-loved and well-trodden myths for us, part of a kind of storytelling of our family. I don't feel this is a challenge to my wish to speak truly and openly – myths are not factual truth but they may speak to a different kind of truth that is also important.

Guin, MBCP meditation teacher and mum of three

I think that the way we tackle Christmas ought to be considered alongside other important questions, such as the beliefs we hold about religion, life and death. When my daughter was almost three our pet chicken died, and I casually mentioned that all beings die eventually. She asked me about people we knew – would they die too? A moment or two later she wailed, 'I don't want to die.' It seemed to me a very significant moment, that this being I had brought into life had come to know of her own mortality.

For me, make-believe was part of the magic of childhood. So I keep that magic in my son's childhood – the idea that anything is possible.

Kate, mum to Zach, 2½

Later I felt that I had perhaps spoken too quickly and with too much certainty. Did I *really* know what was meant by death and dying? And even if I did, was I *really* able to convey a sense of this to my two-year-old daughter, with her limited command of language? I began to wonder if I had presented a belief as truth. Did I know for a fact that everyone would die? Did I know for a fact what would happen after death? No. In later conversations with both my children I have spoken with less conviction, trying not to say more than I know, and inviting them to draw their own conclusions.

BEING FIRM TO BE KIND

At first sight 'speaking kindly' seems to be pretty straightforward. Being kind can be defined as being considerate and benevolent and, I would argue, recognizing someone's value and acting in their best interests. So speaking kindly ought to simply reflect that spirit of well-wishing (see page 43). However, when it comes to our children that can actually be extremely complex. As parents we are perpetually being thrust into uncomfortable situations where it really isn't obvious at all how to be kind. For example, how do you speak (and behave) kindly in the following situations?

- Your child steps into the road without looking.
- Your toddler bites another child.

Being kind is a complex issue, because not only do we need to show our children how much we love and care for them, and to validate their desire to explore and make sense of the world, we also need to act as their protectors, educators and social guides. We also have a duty to protect other people and their possessions from our children too.

Sometimes we need to be firm to be kind. Sometimes we may even need to be quite tough.

- 'Stop! Stepping out into the road is SO dangerous.'
- 'I need to keep other children safe. If you bite, I'll have to take you home.'

Are these sentences kind? I think they can be very kind. Although you may be thwarting your child, and even upsetting him in the short term, these rules of conduct need to be taught in order to keep him (and others) safe. For me, the important test is not so much what we say, or how our child feels, but what *we feel*. Have we spoken our words with anger, or with love?

Whenever I need to be firm or tough with my children, I try to remember to stay *on their side*. Now that doesn't mean agreeing with everything they are doing. Instead it means having their best interests at heart. It may well mean looking at the long-term view along with the short-term. Very often staying on their side also means acknowledging that it is hard for them to do what we ask. So in the above examples we might also say:

- 'I know you were excited to see Daddy over there.'
- 'You got angry when that little girl snatched your car.'

And it's important for us to really acknowledge these reasons too. Understanding why our child has behaved in a certain way helps us to prevent anger rising. Then, when we are mindfully aware of all the factors, we can choose how to get our message across. This doesn't have to take time. We can become mindful in an instant. Sometimes we need to act and speak very fast (take the child stepping into the road). Moments of danger tend to be conducive to mindfulness anyway. Some parents think that we shouldn't raise our voices to our children. However, I would argue that there are times when this is helpful. When there is danger, it is very important to get your child's attention, and also to convey your own sense of urgency. There may be other times, too, when a raised voice gets a message across powerfully. Just check – are you still on your child's side?

REDUCING CHATTER AND UNNECESSARY SPEECH

The next interesting test is whether speech is necessary and timely. When I first came across the idea that I should consider being sparse with my words, I felt rather shocked – as a writer, words are my trade. Why should I limit them? However, when we think about it a little more, I am sure we have all had the experience of being with someone who chats incessantly about mundane matters. It can actually be rather tortuous to find ourselves stuck next to someone like this, perhaps on a plane journey, for example.

A friend once told me that when he was little, his father told him that there were only so many words allotted to each person. When they were used up, that was it, his father said. You wouldn't be able to speak any more. Now this was a rather cruel tactic to reduce the chatter from his children. However, there is something about this idea of having a finite number of words that puts an interesting spin on the way we speak. Imagine how much more careful we would be if we knew that we might reach our limit one day?

This notion came back to me one winter (before I was meditating) when I was suffering from acute laryngitis. I was teaching English at the time and my voice disappeared entirely. I could only whisper, and that in itself was a strain. I remember explaining to my students that I could hardly talk, and they would need to listen carefully. Amazingly, that was one of the most focused classes I have ever led. As soon as I held up my hand to indicate I would speak, the whole class fell into a hush. Because they were so few, my words seemed to really count. At home and socializing, I started to enjoy my imposed silent retreat. I found myself leaning forward to contribute to conversations, and then deciding that actually my comment wasn't worth straining my voice for. If someone else made the point I had thought of, that pleased me rather than irritated me as it meant I didn't need to bother speaking. I started to enjoy not having to try to get a word in edgeways during more heated discussions in the pub. I realized that much of what I say is unnecessary – I simply want to join in the conversation – perhaps even just to get a little attention for myself.

Of course, after a few days my voice came back, and with it my readiness to offer my opinions. But I always remember that illness with fondness because it taught me how staying silent can actually be a comforting state. It feels both safe and judicious. And when we do speak with care, our audience tends to take note.

When our offspring are babies it is easy to talk over them more, as they cannot 'talk' with us. But I have always tried to include Zach in conversation and make sure that, just because he is little, he is not overlooked. Sometimes I have to remind other adults to keep him included in conversations even though he is two and a half! As he can talk now, I remember to talk to him about something to do with him, rather than talk about him in front of him.

Kate, mum to Zach, 2½

LISTENING

I've talked a lot about speaking, but listening is just as important – perhaps more so. I learnt a lot about listening from the classic book *How to Talk so Kids will Listen and How to Listen so Kids will Talk* by Faber and Mazlish.[20] The authors explain how important it is to give children our attention when they are speaking and allow ourselves to really hear what it is they are trying to tell us. So often, they argue, parents fall into the trap of denying children's feelings and experience. ('You can't be hungry; you just ate dinner. You don't want to go home. Look how interesting it is here!') Instead, they suggest that we validate and name our children's experiences. This way they feel heard, and they also become more emotionally literate. The authors wrote this book in 1980, a long time before mindfulness was in vogue. However, even though they don't use the word mindfulness, that's exactly what we need to practise the strategies for listening and speaking that they suggest.

Active listening is about allowing ourselves to make a mindful connection with our children. To really be in their present, and hear what they have to say. Sometimes what they say isn't what we want to hear. In that case, it's so easy to switch off, deny their reality and close down their words. When we establish speaking as a mindful activity, we also naturally incorporate listening. Sometimes listening involves speaking to show (or check) that we have understood; sometimes it simply involves being silent with a shared attention.

My husband showed me a great TED talk recently of a man called Dave Morris teaching improvization. But the talk wasn't just about comedy or music skills – really it was a 10-minute guide to living because (as he put it) 'life *is* an improvization'. Morris came out with a great remark, which really stuck with me – 'Listening is the willingness to change.' He says that if we are not willing to change based on what we hear, then we are not really listening.[21] Change doesn't have to mean changing our identity; it can simply mean having a deeper understanding.

I think this is a great attitude to have toward listening. We listen, not so we can respond with our own ideas, but so we can really find out about people. Listening is a way of expressing our curiosity about life. Daily life around children can involve so much work and responsibility that we forget to be curious about our children. It can feel more important to simply tick the next thing off the 'to do' list than actually allow ourselves to connect and mindfully recognize their – and our – experience.

SUMMARY

- *The incessant voice in our head sometimes repeats old scripts that are no longer relevant or helpful. Shining the torch of mindfulness on them helps us to make a conscious choice about our words.*

- *The more we practise speaking mindfully, the easier it becomes, until speaking itself is a mindful activity.*
- *A useful guide to speech is whether it is true, kind, necessary and timely.*
- *We are only truly listening when we are prepared to change our understanding based on what we hear.*

8

Managing Difficult Behaviour
with Mindfulness

So what does it mean to discipline with mindfulness? Because mindfulness is a quality of mind rather than a set of behaviours, I don't think it's possible to package any particular parenting style as 'mindful', and it wouldn't be appropriate for me to issue you a set of behaviour-management techniques. But mindfulness can certainly help us when we manage our children's behaviour, whatever your take on discipline, and I want to use this chapter to explore how that might work.

OUR RESPONSIBILITY AS PARENTS

As parents we have many varied responsibilities. First and foremost we need to provide for our children's basic need for food, warmth, security and shelter. Equally as important, we need to love them. I explored the different facets of love in Chapter 4. A major tenet of this kind of love is the act of listening to, and accepting, our children as they are right now. Mindfulness helps us to do that.

However, *accepting* does not mean the same thing as *putting up with bad behaviour*. That wouldn't be helpful at all. As parents it's our duty to manage our children's behaviour – as far as we can. A commitment to being mindful may have nothing to do with being permissive. Mindfulness helps us to recognize the reality of a situation and to discern when and how to act.

STAYING AWARE OF THE GOALS OF DISCIPLINE

We can think of discipline as having five main aims:

1. To protect a child's wellbeing.
2. To protect others.
3. To offer guidance.
4. To provide a child with positive boundaries.
5. To provide a child with tools to manage his or her own behaviour.

Mindfulness comes in useful because it can help us to stay aware of these aims, even when we are presented with a challenging situation. It helps us to find a balance between them when they seem to pull in different directions. Let's look at these in more detail.

PROTECTING A CHILD'S WELLBEING

Sometimes children behave in ways that put them at risk. This could be physical danger, such as running into a road, or touching a hot stove. It could be that we need to limit the amount of TV they watch, or ensure that they brush their teeth. It may be something subtler, such as encouraging healthy eating habits or regular exercise.

We need to balance this duty with our children's need to explore, to take reasonable risks and to learn from their mistakes. Much of the job of keeping our children safe is to provide them with a safe environment, so that they can enjoy a large amount of freedom within that. Assessing risk in an environment has much to do with your knowledge of your own child. For example, while a pond may pose an unacceptable level of risk to a just-crawling baby, it may be that your 21-month-old toddler has enough awareness of it to move with caution when nearby. If the water were a river with a fast-flowing current, however, you may think twice before letting your four-year-old play in the vicinity. Your child's ability to navigate danger may change from day to day –

even from hour to hour. Mindfulness can help us evaluate the risk that presents itself *right now*.

Another aspect of keeping children safe is to allow them to assess danger themselves, in a controlled way. For example, most children can judge their own ability to climb on playground equipment. In general, children don't need to be micromanaged. They can only begin to take up responsibility for keeping themselves safe once they are given the opportunity. However, because we adults have a greater understanding of the world, we need to use our judgement to provide rules and guidance to keep them safe from major harm.

Mindfully becoming aware of the different factors at play can help you make a balanced choice. Mindfulness will also help you become aware of any fears or conditioning that you have acquired from your own past, which may be skewing your assessment of the situation.

PROTECT OTHERS

We are also responsible for making sure our children don't harm other people or their property. While children are still learning how to behave acceptably, we need to take reasonable effort to protect others from their mistakes. I use the term *reasonable* effort, because part of the learning experience involves children becoming more independent, and we need to strike a balance between keeping an eye on them and letting them try things for themselves.

However, I think it's clear that we would be derelict in our duties if we allow a child to repeatedly push or hit another child, or if we turn a blind eye to children littering or vandalizing public property, for example. Sometimes, if I am feeling slightly tired and disengaged with my son, it can feel tempting to 'let him get on with' his play, even though I know he is in a destructive and potentially harmful mood. In those cases I drag my feet about intervening, often until it is too late and he has threatened another child. When I am honest with myself I can recognize that I should have got involved much sooner, and helped to disperse bad feeling before it got out of hand.

OFFER GUIDANCE

So why should we correct bad behaviour, if we are supposed to be accepting of it? Actually this isn't such a conundrum. For me the distinction is like this: I accept that my child is acting like this because this moment is a culmination of everything that has gone before. However, what she is doing is not *socially* acceptable, so we need to learn a better way for the future. As her parent, it's my duty to guide her.

We have a duty to teach our children socially acceptable behaviour so that they can participate successfully in society, both now and in the future. For first-time parents, especially those who have been following a very baby-led approach in the first year, it can feel difficult to make the transition to parenting a toddler. Toward the end of the first year, and certainly beyond it, babies start to explore their world and everything in it. Whereas before, your baby's wants basically equalled her needs, this no longer holds true.

Now, when she indicates a desire to pick your neighbour's flowers, we may need to look beyond that want to a deeper need to be taught how to respect other people's possessions.

To a large extent, young children will learn how to behave in an acceptable manner in their own time, simply through following the examples of those around them. Deborah Jackson explores how this works in her book *Letting go as Children Grow*. Children don't need to be tamed; they are born wanting to be social. Even with minimal input from us, they will tend toward the social behaviour they observe.[22]

However, there will be times when you will need to aid this process by giving clear guidance to your child. If you fall short of doing this, then inevitably her uncorrected antisocial behaviour will at some point result in conflict with others. Those others (perhaps other children or critical onlookers) may be less willing to make allowances, and less able to teach acceptable behaviour in a constructive way. Your child's unacceptable behaviour may then lead to her being less popular with others or impede her social development in some other way.

When correcting behaviour, you need to keep in mind what your child is capable of *right now*. Although it may be socially desirable for your two-year-old to sit quietly in a restaurant for the duration of a meal – expecting this type of behaviour would be unrealistic. We can, of course, gently encourage her to stay at the table and use an 'indoor voice', but we need to recognize that her stage of development may mean she is incapable of doing that. It may be more appropriate to try to adjust the environment – perhaps by providing toys or taking her for a walk between courses. Insisting on behaviour that is inappropriate for her age will undoubtedly require great energy and possible conflict. At times like this we can feel very conscious of the expectations of society at large – or perhaps specific people who have an interest in our family.

It won't be necessary for us to dive in and resolve every incident of behaviour that seems in some way undesirable. If it doesn't pose any immediate danger, then it's perfectly fine to take a 'watch and wait' attitude, and see if it clears up by itself. This might be over the course of a few minutes, or it might be over a few years.

Ultimately it's not for me to tell you how to teach your child to behave. Different methods will be appropriate at different times. Perhaps you will gently explain to her that her behaviour is not acceptable. Perhaps (especially if your child is ill or tired or hungry) you may decide that this time it's better to overlook the behaviour without comment. (We are often told to choose our battles wisely.) It may be that you need to be quite forceful with her and use strong words. Only you can judge what is needed in the moment. And you can only do that if you are being mindful of the whole situation – including what emotions her behaviour has triggered in you.

PROVIDE POSITIVE BOUNDARIES

Providing boundaries means different things to different people. I don't mean being very authoritarian, though of course some people do provide boundaries in this way. What I see as the purpose of boundaries is providing a safe, containing space for children to grow and develop with confidence. Positive boundaries are the 'norms' that children can rely on. They can be in the form of everyday routines and habits, such as the physical space in which they play, the time they normally go to bed and so on. This is the framework of their daily lives: 'the way we do things'. It's fine to have some degree of flexibility around these, but complete unpredictability makes it much harder for children to feel secure. Chaotic patterns result in more decision-making, which saps energy from the whole family.

Boundaries can also be set through imposed rules, such as speaking kindly, not harming, not snatching, etc. I think the best kinds of rules are ones that feel self-evident; children can understand and accept them because they seem fair.

It's important that boundaries are not imposed too rigidly, or so often that they stifle children's ability to explore and experiment. I don't think it's helpful if our children fear us as strict authoritarians – unquestioning obedience can come at the expense of playfulness and connection. But it is important that they can rely on us to provide containment: that if they go too far, they can expect us to pull them back. Of course, they probably won't thank us at the time if we are limiting or thwarting them. But hopefully over time, our occasional stepping in to uphold the rules will leave them with the impression that we are firm and fair.

Boundaries are not so much about limiting our children, but about channelling their energy in a constructive direction. Boundaries provide a safe basis for children to explore and develop with confidence. I suspect that a secure, loving environment (that is supported by positive boundaries) in early childhood does much to encourage the equanimity I discussed in Chapter 4 (see page 54). It seems to me that equanimity is the quality of feeling confident and safe, and allows us to rise to the greater challenges that life poses without fear of being overwhelmed. I am sure that absorbing the experience of a safe, orderly world in the early years does much to enable a sense of inner balance and security later on.

Much of the job of setting and maintaining boundaries is about balancing needs. Babies and children demand a great deal from us, and it is up to us to work out when those needs should be met and when we need to put other people (including ourselves) first. Balancing internal and external mindfulness is a big part of this process. Without raising mindfulness of our thoughts and feelings, we cannot assess our needs clearly. Likewise, being aware of the broader picture – the little (and sometimes big) signals that our children are sending off, alongside the expectations and requirements of society, helps us to navigate all the different factors.

HELP THEM TO GOVERN THEIR OWN BEHAVIOUR

Another major aspect to guiding our children is to provide them with the tools they need to regulate themselves. Much of the work of self-discipline is through learning healthy habits and ways to behave in familiar circumstances. We can do much to help our children form these habits – turn-taking, being polite, respecting each other's space and belongings, and so on.

However, real self-discipline is tested when our children face a situation that is new to them, or is so intense that it triggers an angry reaction (say) and learnt behaviours are forgotten. Ultimately, we want our children to remain calm, assess the situation by taking into account all the factors, and decide on the best course of action. This is not an easy task, and mindfulness plays a big part.

One way that you can do this is to encourage your children to work out their own solutions to problems. They will certainly need a lot of help with this. For example, if children are squabbling over a toy, rather than stepping in and declaring they get two minutes each, or confiscating the toy, we can help them resolve it together. This may be by encouraging each child to tell his or her side of the story and listening carefully. You may need to interpret the child's version:

- 'It sounds like you were feeling frustrated because Elsa was taking a long time.'
- 'You felt you had a right to it because you were playing with it first.'

By naming their feelings, you are encouraging them to be mindful of their own internal state and each other's. Once both the children have been heard, and have recognized what they are each feeling, you can encourage them to find a solution.

This kind of approach to discipline requires parents to keep in mind both the short- and long-term goals of parenting. In the short-term, we want to resolve a situation quickly and restore calm, and in the long-term we want to equip our children with the tools to acknowledge difficulties and the means to resolve them.

DISCIPLINING WITH EMPATHY

Maintaining mindfulness as our children scream and hit us can be extremely difficult. For first-time parents, the first experience of our toddler's rage and fury, directed at *us,* can be really upsetting and triggering. It seems surprising and almost hurtful. '*Who stole my loving, gurgling baby?*', you might ask. You might start to question the way you parent: '*Have I been too hard? Have I been too soft?*' You may feel attacked and criticized by onlookers (both real and imagined) and even by your child herself.

Until now, it has been fairly easy to understand your child's behaviour. You have been so well connected and in tune with each other that her emotions are reflected in yours, almost like a mirror. When she feels happy, you also feel happy. When she feels sad, you meet her in that sadness too. This understanding enables you to keep an empathy and warmth between you. But now, as she screams at you, red in the face, because you have taken away the sticky lolly she has picked up from the pavement – or whatever crisis it happens to be – now, she has become a separate entity who is, at this moment, pitted against you. Suddenly, instead of being in harmony with your child, you feel at odds with her.

THOUGHTS THAT UNDERMINE GOOD DISCIPLINE

The intense situations that regularly arise around children can trigger equally intense reactions in us. Thoughts themselves can be incredibly destructive and can prevent us from seeing the reality of the situation. Here are some examples of negative thoughts that impede our ability to think clearly:

- 'My child shouldn't be behaving like this.'
- 'My child shouldn't have to be in this situation.'
- 'I have failed as a parent.'
- 'Other people are judging me.'

Perhaps you recognize some of these. I know I have thought all of them at times! The first two of these thoughts come from a denial about the reality of the situation. We just don't want to admit that it is happening. The problem with this is that if we won't accept the situation as it is, it becomes impossible to respond to it appropriately. Instead we may find ourselves becoming angry, either with our children or the world in general.

The second two thoughts are unhelpful assessments. Instead of looking at the situation non-judgementally, we are putting a particular negative gloss on the situation. If we decide that we have been too lenient in the past, we may seek to redress that right now by being excessively strict. If we allow ourselves to react to our internal thoughts and feelings without first recognizing them, then we will almost certainly fail to address the situation as it actually is.

Sometimes, because I care so much about them, if they
behave badly it makes me much more likely to be angry
than someone else would.

Deborah, meditation teacher and mum to Jesse, 20,
and Rowan, 17

HOW INDEPENDENCE CAN LEAD TO DISCONNECTION

Moments of conflict are an inevitable result of your child's
growing independence. What do I mean by that? I'll show you in
an example:

Sarah is sitting on a playground bench, chatting to a friend. Her
three-year-old son, Tommy, comes running over from the other
side of the playground.

'Can I have a snack?' he asks, tugging her arm.

'Hang on, Tommy, I'm just talking,' she says.

'I WANT A SNACK!' he suddenly starts shouting, and
grabs at Sarah's bag.

Sarah feels utterly embarrassed by his behaviour and can feel
anger rising inside her.

What Sarah doesn't know is what led up to this incident:

Tommy had made a new friend in the playground called Lily,
who had just suggested they go for a snack. Feeling hungry,
Tommy followed her to the far side of the playground, where her
mother pulled out two purple snack bars. Tommy reached out for
one, but instead of giving it to him, Lily's mother passed the extra
bar to another older boy, who had come up behind him. Wrong-
footed and disappointed, Tommy ran back to his mother.

Sarah is unaware of what led up to the outburst, so it is really
hard for her to stay empathic with her son. As our children grow,
and spend more and more time away from us, and more under
the influence of the outside world, we can expect to have less

knowledge of what exactly causes their behaviour. It can be really hard to accept a behaviour when we don't know where it comes from. This can be a key transition in our relationships with our children. *When* it comes will depend on the temperament of your baby, your individual circumstances and your level of mindfulness. But it does happen to all parents. And once it starts to happen, the trick is to try to let it happen less often, and to try to regain the connection as soon as you notice it has been broken.

UNDERSTANDING THE CAUSE OF BAD BEHAVIOUR

What we can be sure of (when we can think about it in a calm moment), is that all of children's behaviour is due to *something*. Bad behaviour doesn't come out of nowhere.

When we are confronted with a screaming or angry child, it's really hard to recall that there must be a reason for this undesirable behaviour. And, actually, this is *not* the moment to be considering possible causes – that can come later, when there is a little more space to think calmly. What *is* required in the moment is just you being present with your child – accepting the situation as it is in the moment. Having a theoretical understanding that all behaviour is due to something, and so therefore all behaviour is reasonable, can help us to be more accepting in the heat of the moment, but it's not always enough. By far and away the most useful thing to help us be mindful in such situations is *habit*. And habit comes through practice.

Every time we are confronted with a challenging situation, we can try to remember that this is the time to be mindful. After a few tries at this, we get better at recognizing flashpoint situations as they start to occur, and we become accustomed to raising mindfulness when they do. You may even find that it is quite easy to raise mindfulness in extreme situations, as the situation itself reminds you to draw on extra resources to help get you through it. It is that act of *remembrance* that is so crucial in maintaining self-awareness. Actually, it is often the less intense situations that catch us out – the whining, or the over-boisterousness, or absentmindedness in our children. I find myself so easily reacting to this kind of subtle negativity, because I am not on red alert, the way I would be if my child were screaming.

A commitment to raising mindfulness at stressful moments can be massively supported by a regular formal practice, which I discuss in more detail in Chapter 12. Formal practice can 'top up' your mindfulness reserves so that it is more available for you at times of need.

It's made me pay deeper attention to what my child is really trying to tell me when, for example, he's angry. I see that bad behaviour is sometimes a call for love or attention, or a way of telling me that I'm on another planet and not present for him, rather than just bad behaviour for the sake of it. On a good day, that means I react more kindly to him, or perhaps engage with him instead of punishing him, which turns things around immediately.

Ben, dad to Leo, 6

ALLOWING BEHAVIOUR VERSUS LETTING THEM GET AWAY WITH IT

Now, as I mentioned before, all this *does not* mean that we allow our children to 'get away' with undesirable behaviour without correction. I think confusion arises because we talk about mindfully 'accepting' whatever is happening in the moment. Clearly, some behaviour is not 'acceptable'. What I mean by mindful acceptance is accepting the way our children are in our core or heart. That sounds a bit wishy-washy, but I think you will know what I mean. A mindfulness teacher I know talks about the spirit of 'allowing'. I think this is also a good word. When we are not mindful, when we don't accept or allow, bad behaviour can make us feel offended. It strikes at our core and makes us want to lash out in retaliation. ('Don't you dare speak to me like that!') This is the opposite of acceptance. It is a *rejection* of who our children are being at this moment. Now that's a big, bad word to use in conjunction with our children. No parent wants to think they are rejecting their child. But if we look closely, when we feel offended by our children's behaviour that is exactly what we are doing.

Now, of course, we all do this at times. But it doesn't make us feel good, and it doesn't make our children feel good. Our knee-jerk reaction may teach them that Mum or Dad gets angry when they speak like that, but it will also make them feel misunderstood and attacked. And the situation is very likely to escalate. In these cases, I find that if the shouting or crying rockets to the point that I start searching around for tools to help me, and I suddenly remember to be mindful again, then, I'm able to start making things better, not worse.

Often bad behaviour does need guidance; but if we are *allowing* our children to be who they are in this moment, then we can guide them from the standpoint of *being on their side*.

WILL MY CHILD TAKE ME SERIOUSLY IF I'M NOT ANGRY?

This is an issue I struggle with. The truth of the matter is that when we are angry, and our children hear that in our words, they *do* take us seriously. Of course, what they learn when they are feeling afraid or rejected is not necessarily what we want our children to learn. Learning obedience is not the same as learning co-operation. It can be hard to sound firm when we are not angry.

However, by repeatedly holding steadfast, and calmly but firmly repeating your message, your child should eventually learn that you mean business, even if you have not resorted to shouting.

WHAT BEHAVIOUR TOOLS CAN I USE?

I have read many parenting books, and many of them argue for and against different behavioural strategies. For a long time I allied myself with some of these theories of behaviour management, and ruled out certain strategies. Eventually I came to see that I was unnecessarily limiting myself, and making myself feel disempowered.

For example, I was suspicious of using sticker charts. But after a while I wondered if using one might help my daughter make more effort over some issue. I forget now what it was, but perhaps she was resorting to shouting too much. I drew up a chart of the week and armed myself with some stick-on stars. Around the same time, she pointed out that I was also getting stressed too often. I playfully suggested that I ought to have a chart too – and get a star every day I didn't get stressed.

TIP: Discipline strategies

So while you don't necessarily need to use the full range of discipline strategies available, try not to rule any of them out. Instead when faced with a new situation, look honestly and pragmatically at all the tools available and try to choose a method of discipline that supports both your short- and long-term goals of parenting.

So we both embarked on our sticker chart journey, and I can honestly say that for the couple of weeks that we kept it up, it made a massive difference to how we both behaved – especially me! The chart really motivated me and encouraged me to be more mindful in my speech and helped me not get as stressed.

It may be that the idea of doing a sticker chart for yourself is repellent – and of course I'm not suggesting that you have to do it! But I do think that as a rough rule of thumb, we should use behaviour management strategies on our children that we would be happy for them to use on us. Also, if you have (or are planning to have) more children, your older ones will almost certainly use your discipline methods as a model for the way they relate to their younger siblings. For me, this is perhaps the most significant reason why I would not use physical violence against my children as a form of discipline.

Sometimes, as unpleasant as it is, you have to tune in to the
fact that kids are not yet fully developed and depending
on their personality some of their behaviour is unskilful
and that is not something they can change in an instant.
Jan, mum to Josia, 8 and Hannah, 5

BEING AUTHENTIC WITH OURSELVES

I found that being prepared to make use of a wider range of
strategies meant that I was better equipped to tackle behaviours
that were worrying me. Sometimes I have held back from, for
example, insisting that my daughter wear warm clothes, because
I have been worried about imposing my will on her. Sometimes I
have let my son stay up too late because I don't feel strong enough
to bear the tantrum I am expecting.

The problem with not acting, when we know we should in our
heart of hearts, is that this can really undermine our confidence.
If we pretend that the situation is fine, when really we know it's
not, then we are not being authentic. This can also send out a
subtle message to our children that we are weak, and that we don't
respect our own ability to discern what's right and wrong. If we
send this message out repeatedly, it can lead children to feel that
they are growing up in a world without boundaries – where no
one is in charge.

These situations can come up when we have lost confidence in
our usual strategies for persuading our children to behave. It is so
easy to get stuck on one way of doing things that we can't think
of alternatives when the old way stops working. It is far better to
experiment with a new approach than it is to do nothing at all.

I recently had a horrible long journey in the car with my
son and made some risky manoeuvres that I regret. Since
then I have decided to have one CD permanently in the

car that I switch on if I feel at all stressed driving. It's there to calm us down and remind me to be mindful while I'm driving. My life and his is too precious to risk getting stressed at the wheel.

Emily, mum to Owen, 2

TIP: Work out strategies in advance (or for next time)

When we are confronted with a new or particularly tricky situation, the need to act quickly and decisively may make it hard to choose the absolute best course of action in that moment. Of course, in an ideal world, we would be able to pre-empt the situation and decide in advance how we might manage it. In reality however, we can't predict every flashpoint. When an intense situation arises, or your child has an extreme reaction to something, then you have to weather it as best you can at the time.

Later, however, when things have calmed down, we can see the incident as a learning opportunity. It has brought to light that something is out of kilter. Rather than getting caught up in blame or regret, this is a great opportunity to think how we can handle the situation differently next time. Next time round, we can be prepared.

When we have a chance to think through what strategies might work best in particular circumstances, we have the opportunity to mindfully consider the specific needs of our own child – rather than just adopt the first strategies that come to mind. This means that we don't necessarily need to discipline or set boundaries in the same way that our parents or friends did. Instead we can choose the tactic that will work for our own child, right now.

DISCIPLINING YOUR CHILDREN IN PUBLIC

Dealing with children who are being disruptive or having a tantrum can be hard enough as it is, but if you add a crowded venue to the occasion, or perhaps some unsympathetic relatives, then the situation can feel acutely challenging.

Trying to stay connected to your child while dealing with bad behaviour, at the same time as acknowledging the needs of the adults in the vicinity, can feel like an impossible task. Feeling like you are being observed, and worse, *judged*, can make it extremely difficult to keep your equanimity at times of stress. You feel 'got at' from all sides, and it's very hard to see clearly. For many parents, the gaze of onlookers makes them more inclined to be tough on their kids. The negative thoughts I mentioned earlier in the chapter rise up sharply: *You shouldn't be behaving like this; I've let you get spoilt.* Thoughts like these take hold of our minds and can cause intense anger. But, unfortunately, it is very unlikely that an angry reaction will be the most effective way to move forward in the situation.

It may even be that there is some truth in the thought that your child needs some firmer boundaries. However, the heat of the moment is almost certainly not the optimal time to introduce them!

I'm mindful of how my reaction to my child changes when he is acting badly in front of other adults. I may be harsher with him than I would be if we were alone, and I see that this is because I'm more worried about the judgement of others toward me as a parent, than his actual behaviour. So I try to moderate this behaviour in myself now, and treat him the same way whether he is misbehaving at home with us, or when others are around.

Ben, dad to Leo, 6

STAYING CALM, WHEN OTHERS THINK WE SHOULD BE ANGRY

Trying to sustain mindfulness during public outbursts can be very difficult, but we need to keep our presence of mind if we want to continue to be the parents we want to be. In Chapter 2 (see page 23) I mentioned how I used my daughter's scream as a bell of mindfulness. This was particularly useful when it started ringing in public. I began to try to see these moments when my daughter had caused a public spectacle and I had been 'called on the stage', as opportunities to try out my best parenting skills. It wasn't that I arrogantly thought I had all the answers and wanted to show off to other parents. I just wanted to make sure that I was presenting myself in a way I could be proud of – or at least not regret later.

Just yesterday, I was out for a walk down a farm track with my four-year-old son. An older lady passed within earshot just as my son said to me, rather indecorously, 'Come ON, Mum. And bring my bike.' I noted his rudeness, but I didn't feel angry. He is normally quite considerate, and on this occasion he was excited to examine a piece of fencing. As the purpose of our walk was to have some quality time together, I saw fit to let it pass, and I simply did as he bade. However, as I smiled a greeting to the lady walking by, I could see her mouth turn down with obvious disapproval, directed at both my son and myself.

Staying patient and connected while disciplining your child is extremely hard work. When adults around me are critical – not just of my child's behaviour, but actually of my *patience*, then that makes it even harder. The very thing I am trying so hard to do – maintain my mindfulness and equanimity while I work out the best course of action – is what they see as the problem. These adults may be so angered by my child's behaviour that they want to see me lash out, lose my cool and 'teach my child a lesson'.

It is really hard sometimes not to be influenced by these attitudes. I personally don't find it too hard to brush off the opinions of strangers. If the lady on the farm track really was as angered by our behaviour, as I guessed from her expression, then ultimately, she simply deserves my compassion. I find it much harder to maintain my equilibrium when I feel undermined by people I know. However, it is important that we tease out judgemental attitudes and unrealistic expectations and see them for what they really are – whether those come from within us, or from external sources in the form of onlookers.

BEING MINDFUL ABOUT THE NEEDS OF OTHER PEOPLE

We do, however, need to take into account the opinions of the people around us, especially if our child's behaviour is negatively impacting on them. One time, my daughter threw a tantrum on a crowded bus. I spent the entire journey steadfastly silent, vowing to myself that I would set out expectations of behaviour to my daughter so that this never happened again. But later I realized that I could have done much more to acknowledge the needs of the other passengers on the bus. At the time I had felt myself to be a victim of circumstances. My mindfulness only extended so far as to keep myself from getting angry, and to consider how I would prevent this reoccurring. Instead of recognizing that my daughter must be causing the other passengers to have a really unpleasant journey, feeling compassion for them and apologizing generally, I disconnected myself from them. The truth was that I didn't feel responsible for my daughter's outburst – I felt that I was suffering from it too. I knew that there was very little I could do to actually quiet her (besides dragging her off the bus). If I had been able to conjure a little more equanimity, I might have been able to be more generous.

TALKING WITH CHILDREN ABOUT BEHAVIOUR

Talking with children about their own behaviour and behaviour in general is absolutely crucial to helping them learn how to manage it better themselves. When we get into the habit of doing this, it also helps us to think about what's really going on, rather than just reacting.

TEACHING CHILDREN TO CHECK THEIR INTENTION

If we are not fully connected with our children, it is very easy to be critical of their surface behaviour, and not take the time to look a bit deeper inside. When I'm childminding I regularly find that one child complains to me about the actions of another: 'She keeps following me.' 'He keeps tapping my foot.' 'She's singing too loudly.' At these times the complaining child wants me to step in and tell the other child not to behave in an annoying way. If I'm not paying enough attention, sometimes I will simply go along with it and tell the child to stop tapping/singing/following or whatever it is.

The problem with this approach is that it is very likely that *both* children were in some way provoking the other, but the 'complaining' child has been smart enough to keep within the accepted rules. The 'annoying' child will then most likely complain – 'But I was *only* singing,' or will find some way to get around the rule, and annoy the child in another way.

I have come to realize that it's far more important to pay attention to the *intention* of the behaviour, rather than the behaviour itself. And encouraging the children to do that helps them to regulate their own behaviour. So, now (when I remember), I say something like: '*Following* is allowed, but what is *not* acceptable is deliberately trying to make someone else unhappy. So you both need to check inside yourself *why* you are doing that, to see if it's OK or not.' I point out to them that they can use their own feeling as a guide to their behaviour.

Normally both children will find my answer dissatisfying. The one making the original complaint was hoping I would back him up, so he would have the upper hand in the argument. The 'annoying' child has had his motive brought to light – he can't continue playing the game by finding loopholes (*'she never said I couldn't hum.'*) However, repeatedly taking this strategy teaches children to work a bit harder to learn how to regulate themselves. Children prefer to have black and white rules – they don't have to think about it, and they can find loopholes. If they get used to using their intentions as a guide, then they can transfer this mode of regulation to any situation.

GOOD GUYS AND BAD GUYS

My son came across the idea of 'good guys' and 'bad guys' during a period of watching too much TV, and the concept has firmly stuck. Much of his play revolves around these two sets of people fighting. Now as much as I might prefer him to play less aggressively, I can see that he is using this type of play to work through feelings about himself and the way he interacts with the world. I can also see that my son is not unusual in his interest – 'good guys' and 'bad guys' seem to capture the imagination of most children, and they like the simplicity of viewing the world through this lens.

In my son's play there are equal levels of violence from both the 'good guys' and the 'bad guys'. The 'good guys', however, seem to have some kind of moral standpoint that sanctions their behaviour.

In time, I think that it is right to help children understand that people are not simply 'good' and 'bad'. It is very hard for children to appreciate that people only act in certain ways because of the culmination of what has gone on before. Frankly, it's hard enough for us to remember it at times too! And we are up against some very powerful messages from popular culture, which likes to lay blame and seek revenge.

But even quite young children can understand the distinction between 'being bad' and 'doing bad acts'. I have tried to explain to my children that people are only good or bad through doing good or bad things, and that they always have the choice between those options.

When someone stole our bicycle with Zach's child seat recently, he was upset. I wanted to tell him a nasty person took the bike but then remembered that is spreading more hate, so I just said a big boy took it because he himself felt sad about something. Somehow this felt right and true. Then my partner joined the discussion and joked: 'Let's get revenge!' The next thing I knew my son was shouting: 'Revenge! Gimme my bike back big boy!' It made me laugh, but I still preferred my method!

Kate, mum to Zach, 2½

SUMMARY

- *'Disciplining with mindfulness' does not mean you have to follow a specific set of techniques.*
- *There are five main reasons why we need to manage our children's behaviour: to protect their wellbeing; to protect others; to offer guidance; to provide them with positive boundaries; to provide them with tools to manage their own behaviour.*
- *Understanding that there are causes of bad behaviour can help us to maintain empathy. This helps us mindfully accept our children's challenging behaviour, while at the same time helping us see how we can address it.*
- *Raising mindfulness at times of stress takes practice, but before long, mindfulness can become our habitual response to extreme scenarios.*
- *When children behave badly in public it can be even harder to stay mindfully connected to them. We need to see past unhelpful thoughts, yet also stay aware of other people's needs.*

Chapter 9

Managing Challenging Feelings in Ourselves

Not long ago I lost a person whom I loved. The loss absolutely struck me down, and I was astonished by the raw intensity of my feelings. It had not been wholly unexpected – in fact it had been preceded by several months of fearing the worst. However, no amount of anticipation could have prepared me for its devastating effects.

I felt as if I had been ripped apart and left to be swept about on tides of helpless anxiety, anger and despair, sometimes so engulfing that I literally couldn't hold myself upright. Sometimes the pain in my chest was so tight that I could barely answer my children's questions, and I found myself sneaking away so that I could hide in my bed and cry. I had no idea how I could look after myself, and at the same time 'be there' for my children.

WEATHERING STRONG EMOTIONS

These kinds of difficult feelings – anger, depression, anxiety and grief – to a greater or lesser extent, come to all of us at times. When they do, they can be frightening and overwhelming. This is where a mindfulness practice can be *invaluable* in helping you weather the storm – and, eventually, to heal. In fact, challenging times met with mindfulness can be an opportunity for growth – and the bigger the challenge, the more the potential for insight. My struggle to come to terms with what had happened, and the deep feelings that it aroused, taught me a huge amount about myself, my practice and life in general. It was as if I had been unexpectedly enrolled in a crash course on dealing with difficult feelings – but there wasn't a teacher or textbook.

But it can be extremely difficult to navigate such strong emotions at the same time as trying to look after your children. Our thoughts may be so engrossed by the subject of our anguish that we can't concentrate on our children, or we may be so sapped of energy that even the simplest of tasks seem insurmountable. Over time I came to learn what coping strategies helped me to ease my own pain, and enabled me to function as best I could as a parent.

TIP: Giving your emotions attention

The best way to ensure that you acknowledge difficult feelings as they arise is to bring mindfulness to bear on them, ideally before they mutate into something else and trigger unhelpful thoughts and action. Sometimes this task can be so subtle and complex, that it really requires our full attention. That's why, if you are experiencing strong emotions, it makes sense to allow periods of time for processing them each day.

MAKING TIME TO EXPERIENCE FEELINGS

Before experiencing grief, I had previously thought that the phrase 'time to grieve' meant that one would heal in time – i.e. over several months, or whatever. What I hadn't appreciated is that grieving is actually *time-consuming*. That is, you need to allow actual minutes in the day for experiencing the pain. I came across an article recently that suggested scheduling in an hour a day for mourning. Although I was amused by the business-like approach, it still made sense.

TIP: Allow emotions to surface

Having quiet periods for allowing pain to surface helps in two ways. Firstly, it gives space for the pain, and afterwards, we may feel a little lighter, as if we have worked something through. Or in other words, we get a bit of a break, until next time. Also, by giving it some time and attention, we get to learn what triggers it, and how it might manifest. We get practised at recognizing it and acknowledging it, rather than letting it carry us away into unskilful thoughts and actions. That means that when it does arise at other, less convenient times, we become more adept at recognizing and acknowledging it then too.

It can actually be quite hard work grieving. And, as I found, if you don't acknowledge your pain, it can mutate into something else. For me, that was most often anger or irritation. If I felt an unpleasant sensation arise in me, but I didn't recognize it as grief, then I would look for explanations or solutions ('*This house is so messy*', '*We're going to be late*', '*We aren't earning enough money*').

THE BENEFITS OF ALLOWING TIME

I didn't schedule set periods, but after a few weeks, I noticed that there were certain periods in my day – quieter periods – when I let down my defences and allowed painful feelings to surface. Perhaps the most regular of these was while I put my son to bed at the end of each day. As I lay down with him and cuddled him to sleep, and the room was quiet, then I was able to 'touch in' to the tensions in my body, and investigate them.

I often found it difficult – frightening even – to allow myself to experience the pain in its pure form. I suppose I was frightened that it would be too much for me. I found that becoming very aware of the physical sensations – often a tightness in my chest or sometimes an ache, or a pain in my stomach – would help me to experience it without over-intellectualizing it. The trouble with thoughts is that they often led down distressing alleyways, generating more anxiety or anger. Eventually I learnt to welcome the pain when it came, recognizing that embracing it was the only way to move through it.

When I experience a difficult emotion being very present, or causing me pain or sadness, I 'take it for a walk', meaning that I'll go for a long, mindful walk, being very present for the physical feelings of whatever I'm going through. Usually by the end of the walk the sadness, or pain, has dissolved, and I have some insight into what has caused it. I really find that this is a 'miracle of mindfulness'.

Ben, dad to Leo, 6

GRIEF AS ANOTHER CHILD

Sometimes, grief arose in me, but circumstances didn't allow me to take time out. It often happened when too much was going on. For example, both children might be clamouring, the kettle is boiling and I'm trying to unload the washing. It was as if the challenging feeling was itself another small child pulling my trouser leg, trying to get my attention. If I wasn't being mindful, I found that the pain manifested as an irritant, and I would feel harassed and might snap at whoever was asking for my attention. This made me feel guilty too.

So as soon as I noticed what was happening, I would try to give myself some space. If I wasn't able to *literally* escape, I would try to reduce the number of demands on me. With mindfulness, I could pause, take stock and see where I could limit activities. That might mean prioritizing and finishing activities, or putting them on hold, or explaining to my children that I needed to listen to them one at a time.

You may not be able to pick up this small child (who is your grief) straight away. But even just catching his eye and letting him know you've noticed him will help tide him over, until you can have some quality time together. And when you are able to have regular quality time with him, that may allow him to feel confident enough to play in the other room, so to speak, at times when you cannot give him your full attention. Of course, it's not the grief that feels confident: it's you. When you make time for difficult feelings, you feel more confident that you are taking care of yourself, and that can help to make you stronger throughout the day.

GRIEF AS BIRTH

The process of mourning reminded me a lot of labouring. Like labour contractions, the pangs of grief come in waves – sometimes taking us by surprise. Fighting them, or ignoring them, causes us intense suffering. It is only by surrendering to them that we can render them harmless. And, as with labour pains, the pains of grief are productive. They take us on a journey. Though unlike labour pains, which build in intensity and frequency, grief pains tend to become less intense and more sporadic in time. As in the early stages of labour, there are times in grief, when it is better to allow ourselves to be distracted and not focus on the pangs out of habit. At other times, we absolutely need to allow the process to occur with our awareness, so that it can unfold naturally.

The resonances with labour led me to wonder whether grief itself is a kind of birth process – a kind of growing up – as we learn to be separated from our loved one, and are reborn into a fuller kind of person. And, of course, though we don't normally think of it in those terms – birth is also a process of separation for mother and baby.

INTENSE EXPERIENCES AS A MAGNIFYING GLASS ON LIFE

But I don't want to sound too mystical about the connection between birth and grieving. I think perhaps the reason these experiences have similar elements is simply to do with the fact that they are *part of life*. When we go through very intense experiences, it is as if someone is holding a magnifying glass up to our challenges – not only are they blown up to extreme proportions, but, also, we are forced to look at them.

Actually, we face these types of challenges throughout life, though normally on a much smaller scale. Because when we are feeling harassed or stressed or anxious or depressed, aren't these just reactions to a deeper underlying fear that we've lost our footing somehow? That somehow our inner selves are not being recognized or validated – either by people or by circumstances? So we try to assert ourselves – and regain our footing. But we tend to do that by denying the reality of what's around us and working at odds with it.

Just as with the bigger events, it is our fear of surrender – of *allowing* life to be how it actually is, that creates stickiness and conflict. So instead we complain, or snap, or retreat into ourselves. And this strategy can go unnoticed much of the time. But when we are faced with something bigger – some major challenge, then we have to revaluate how we interact with reality, because fighting it will cause such exhaustion and pain that it will no longer be viable as a strategy.

When enormous difficulties came my way, meditation gave me a refuge, not to be consumed by the problem and sadness but to know I could abide in a space or place where I was free from it like any other person who did not share my problem. And having that place to recharge was of immeasurable help.

Anne, mum to Stephen, 24, Clare, 24, Helen, 23, and Sarah, 20

MEDITATION PRACTICE:
Staying mindful – taming the horse

When I was going through a period of particularly high anxiety, and I felt that I was spiralling out of control, I found it very hard to maintain any mindfulness that I was able to conjure up, instead my self-awareness would quickly slip into self-judgement at my own inability to be mindful. Finally, I came up with a strategy that was slightly off the wall.

When I notice that my mind has become very agitated, and the simple noticing of the fact is not enough to calm it down, I call to mind a horse. I imagine that the horse is acting out my feelings and agitated mind state. Somehow I find it very easy to imagine a big stallion rearing up, snorting and frothing at the mouth. And I imagine myself as the horse's keeper, standing next to it, sometimes waiting patiently, sometimes calling out to it, sometimes whispering soothing words, pressing my fingers into its flank, stroking its thick, oily fur.

I find this visualization very powerful and effective. It redirects the mental energy away from the troubling chain of thoughts and into the creative activity of imagining the horse. It also allows me to rouse the helpful feelings of compassion, love and equanimity – or whatever is needed toward the horse, instead of self-criticism and judgement. When the horse is a little calmer, I can draw closer, and eventually encourage it to nuzzle my shoulder and I can bury my face in its neck.

MINDFUL DOES NOT EQUAL HAPPY

For a very long time after I found out about mindfulness, I had the impression that mindfulness somehow cancelled out negative feelings. I thought that if I were mindful, then I would feel happy, or at least neutral. I was really wrong about this! I was kind of shocked to discover in my grief that mindfulness does not equal happiness. It is perfectly possible to be both mindful and sad because some pains are an intrinsic part of life. But that's not to say that there is no point to mindfulness. A friend recently reminded me of a quotation from Huraki Murakami: 'Pain is inevitable, suffering is optional.' What mindfulness can do is allow us to embrace those hurts without fighting them, so that when they eventually pass through us – with all their terrible pain, we find that they have left no lasting damage. In fact, they may even have left something positive that was not there before – a depth and a humility, and a quiet resilience that enables us to look forward.

TIP: Bringing emotions into the open

Sometimes mental pain will limit the way we interact with our children. At such times it may be useful to explain to them that we are not feeling very well, so we can't play as much as we would like. Of course, it's also important that we don't start to hide behind this image of ourselves, and withdraw from our children when we *are* able to rise to the occasion – I just mean be kind and honest with yourself. Not being able to perform at 100 per cent does not make you a bad parent. We can still be present with them, even if we can't do everything that they, or we, would like.

ACCEPTING HOW YOU FEEL

At first I found it really difficult to accept that I was sad. As a sad mum, I wasn't able to be jolly and creative with the children. I inwardly groaned when my four-year-old cast me as a superhero in his make-believe games. It was so tiring keeping up the pretence. After a while I realized that it's OK to be sad and that not all parents have the good fortune to be in perfect physical or mental health. But I do not believe that this makes them deficient as parents. Of course our children love it when we jump with them on the trampoline – but being able to do that is not the essence of being a good parent.

A few years ago a friend of mine broke her foot. She was a really active mother – she regularly carried her youngest in a sling and they cycled to groups and activities every day. She was in a cast and on crutches for around six weeks. Of course, she was limited in what she could do over those weeks – but she was still able to be a parent to her kids. In her case it helped that her limitations were clearly apparent to both herself and her children. Although it must have been frustrating at times, they could all make allowances, and, to a large extent, even the children avoided feeling affronted when their mum couldn't do her normal activities.

In the early weeks I was dealing with intermittent low mood that would arise every few days, hang around all day and then often be gone the next morning. This was to do with my son's birth reactivating sadness about a previous loss, and it was very difficult to feel preoccupied with this loss at a time when I felt I should be available for getting to know my new baby. It helped enormously to be able to see these low moods from a mindfulness perspective, as passing clouds. Whenever one arrived I focused on treating myself kindly to get through that day, knowing the cloud would lift again soon. I believe this helped me avoid a descent into postnatal depression.

Guin, MBCP meditation teacher and mum of three

MODELLING INNER WORK

Much of the inner work that goes on while you work through challenging emotions will go completely unnoticed by your children. However, I still think that it is worth bearing in mind what we are modelling to our children. How would we want our children to deal with the circumstances and mental states that we find ourselves in? Being kind to ourselves, accepting our limitations and working within them – these are all the kinds of things that we would like to see our children doing in time.

Although they may not be able to see exactly what is going on, and it may not be appropriate to tell them everything, they will still be able to sense the deep self-respect that you emanate as you allow yourself to experience your own feelings. Demonstrating to them that adults feel sad and cry too, but that these feelings are not catastrophic, can be an important lesson. They will see for themselves how the feelings do pass, and that moments of connection – perhaps when your partner or child gives you a hug can make them easier to bear.

Regular meditation was challenging when I was doing a lot of travelling for work. After suffering from depression I eventually felt it necessary to change jobs. That brought a lot of benefits. It's hard to unpick whether routine-focused meditation has been a cause or effect in these changes, but it's definitely part of the story.
Ed, dad to Ruth, 9

MAKING MISTAKES AND PUTTING THINGS RIGHT

It's also important to model mistake-making – and how to put things right. So whenever you do lose your inner equilibrium and act in a way you regret, you have a wonderful opportunity to model moving forward and repairing the damage. Children make a lot of mistakes, so these types of demonstrations are invaluable. Having an inner template of how to make amends can help children to avoid internalizing a sense of failure, which can stop them from moving forward. If you are ultra-judgemental about your own mistakes and apologize profusely, or instead feel even angrier and resentful, then this sends the message that mistakes are intolerable – whether they are yours, or your children's.

SUMMARY

- *All parents experience strong emotions at times. Mindfulness can be a way to help you weather the storm.*
- *Intense emotions such as grief can tug at your attention in the same way another child might. Allowing yourself time to mindfully experience strong feelings can help to prevent them from mutating into stress, irritability and despair.*
- *Being open to strong feelings can provide an opportunity for growth. Our usual strategies for coping with life may no longer be adequate. When we can no longer distract ourselves, we have to learn how to accept and work with difficult states.*
- *Being limited by mental pain does not make a worse parent, just as a physical illness or disability does not. Acknowledging limits (but not hiding behind them) provides a great model for your children.*

10

Supporting Mindful Parenting Through Ethical Living

I was in two minds about whether to include a chapter on ethical living. Is it beyond the scope of this book? Do I have any right to 'preach' to parents about living ethically? But the more I thought about it, the more I realized that not only does our mind-state affect our behaviour, but it also works the other way round: the way in which we behave affects our state of mind. It's a vicious, or virtuous, circle depending on the way we play it. Ultimately our actions are extremely important – and we have to learn how to take full responsibility for them. I realized that avoiding a discussion of ethical behaviour would make this book less useful. But don't worry – I'm not going to preach.

HOW OUR CHILDREN ENCOURAGE US TO 'BE GOOD'

I think that most people revaluate the way they behave once they become parents. For example, most parents would try to avoid or reduce swearing in the presence of a child – even if swearing was previously habitual. Why do we do that? Even if we haven't really considered it, I think we are guided by a couple of factors:

- We tend to have a sense that children, and especially babies, are 'innocents', and we shouldn't 'defile' them with crude language. That sounds a bit unscientific, but it is encapsulated in the sentiment 'it just feels wrong'.

- We are aware that our children are learning from us, and are apt to copy our behaviour and language. When young children do occasionally utter a swear word, it can be really shocking. Or, it might seem so incongruous that it strikes us as being terribly funny.

Now I have used swearing as an example here – but I think this simple example could be extended to all kinds of behaviour. In the main, parents have a natural inclination to behave better around their children, because we want to set a good example to them, and also because of some inner sense that they should not be corrupted.

I also think there is an element of our wanting our children to think we are 'good people'. Because they look up to us, we want to live up to their expectations. Very young children will not judge us, however; it would not occur to them to feel pride or shame. Yet their very being inspires us to do our best. And, in time, they will become more critical of our behaviour. (My seven-year-old regularly pulls me up. Last week I was quick to become exasperated at what I deemed an unreasonable and untimely request for some craft items, and she replied, hurt, 'Mum, I think you could have said that normally.') Even if we don't actively acknowledge it, the idea that we might disappoint them can be a powerful motivator.

Another sentiment common to parents is the idea that we want to try to make the world a better place for our children. At times, especially in the face of some injustice or crime, we may feel powerless to do anything positive. At other times this translates into a desire to do whatever we can.

All of these factors mean that we have a great head start if we want to try to act in ways that help us to be mindful. The problem with bad behaviour – whether it's swearing in front of the kids, being rude to a cold caller, getting drunk and sleeping on a mattress in a skip (a friend of mine did this once), or something worse – is that, quite apart from the harm these actions may do to other people, they leave our minds ruffled and agitated. We are left feeling cross, or het up, guilty or ashamed.

I once went to a talk by Thich Nhat Hanh where somebody asked him a question about karma.[23] The way he explained it really chimed with me. He said that the moment we do something unskilful – say an unkind word, perhaps – in that moment there is an equal and opposite reaction. The harm that we are projecting outward also impacts inward, damaging us. That's karma. So, although the action *may* go out and cause consequences for us in the future (which would also be karma), what is certain is that it will have an immediate negative impact on the do-er in the here and now, too.

The fact is that it's really hard to be mindful when we are brooding over something or feeling guilty or aggrieved or angry. And these are the feelings that tend to accompany unskilful – or we could say, unethical – behaviour. (More about these terms in a minute.) Take anger, for example: Buddhist teaching likens anger to holding a hot coal with the intention to throw it – it *may* hurt your enemy, but it will certainly burn your own hand in the process.

If I had got very angry about something or acted in a way that I knew wasn't a good idea, it would come up in my meditation and clearly be a disturbance to my mind. So I began to realize the power of actions and how unskilful actions agitate and disturb long after they have been done.

Anne, mum to Stephen, 24, Clare, 24, Helen, 23, and Sarah, 20

This is why Buddhism offers an ethical framework – a code to live by. Its main purpose is not to protect others (although it does do this); it's to keep us from harming ourselves. It's a set of rules that can be followed whether you are Buddhist or not, as it has nothing to do with upholding a religion. In fact, most of the rules – or *precepts* (see opposite) – are found in other religious ethical codes – some of them are upheld by common law.

Buddhist precepts

I undertake the training rule to:

- Refrain from killing.
- Refrain from taking what is not given.
- Refrain from sexual misconduct.
- Refrain from false speech.
- Refrain from intoxicants that cause heedlessness.

The Buddhist precepts are not laws, which if broken will incur punishment. Instead they are intentions. By 'taking the precepts', that is reciting them or agreeing to live by them, practitioners acknowledge that the rules help them improve themselves.

I think it is very interesting that all of the rules consist of some kind of abstinence. We are asked to refrain from unhelpful behaviour. I find the precepts really useful. Instead of seeing them as restrictions that are imposed on me, I see them as guiding principles that keep me safe. *If you follow the rules, you will come to no harm* – but not in the sense that I will avoid punishment – I mean that the principles themselves keep me safe from harm. Of course, following them won't stop other people from harming me, but they do keep me from inflicting harm upon myself. And, in fact, when we are behaving well ourselves, we are less likely to incur bad behaviour from other people too.

When we are being truly mindful, actually we don't need to follow rules. When we have a high degree of awareness, it is clear to us what the right action or words should be. But the precepts are a kind of nod toward the fact that we *aren't always* completely mindful. We are not yet perfect beings. That's why they are called 'training rules' because we are still in training. We can see them as a kind of fall back, when the first line of defence – mindfulness – is not fully present. Or perhaps as a reminder to be especially mindful at these times. In fact, in Buddhism they are seen as a necessary foundation for mindfulness. Without a basis of ethical living, it is very difficult to develop mindfulness in the first place.

I think that a practice that focuses on *metta* (loving-kindness) and the other *brahmaviharas* (compassion, sympathetic joy and equanimity) can have a direct ethical impact. It's a more practical way of working toward 'good behaviour' than merely recalling and intending to live by lists of ethical rules or guidelines – such as the Buddhist five precepts or noble eightfold path, or those from other traditions like the Quaker testimonies of peace, equality, simplicity and truth.

Ed, dad to Ruth, 9

THE RELEVANCE OF THE BUDDHIST FIVE PRECEPTS

I think most people would agree that not killing or stealing are unequivocally 'good things'. As far as I know, every society in the world enshrines these basic principles in law. (Though they are sometimes laid aside for the purposes of warfare and punishment.)

But what about the other precepts? At first glance they seem rather strict.

I think we have to understand that they are not so much a moral obligation as a method to keep our minds free from agitation, and to help aid our mindfulness.

REFRAINING FROM SEXUAL MISCONDUCT

If I felt strange bringing up the topic of ethics in the first place, then I definitely feel uneasy talking about sexual misconduct! But I think that reticence comes from something coy within me – because sex is actually an important subject when we are considering how to apply mindfulness within the family. We couldn't have a family without sex. Buddhist rules about sex are to do with preserving trust and intimacy within an established relationship and to avoid causing harm by treading on someone else's toes. The basic rules on sex are don't be unfaithful to your own partner, and don't have sexual relations with someone else's partner.

I don't think that it is hard to see how following that rule of thumb will preserve harmony and connection within the family. Acting on sexual impulses that break these rules can cause a lot of confusion and pain, even if transgressions are not discovered. I think sexual misconduct is included in the precepts, not to be prudish, but to recognize the fact that sexual impulses can be very strong, making mindfulness harder. So we are reminded to be extra careful around sexual matters.

REFRAINING FROM FALSE SPEECH

Most of us will teach our children not to lie. When it comes to ourselves, however, we may often fudge the rules a bit and utter a 'white lie' to save someone's feelings, or to avoid conflict. A couple of years ago, I was at a festival with some friends and their school-age child. They wanted to stay over Sunday night, but were worried about how the school would react. 'Couldn't you just say she's ill?' I suggested. My friend said, 'I could, but I prefer not to lie.' Her answer called to my attention the casualness with which I had suggested lying. I was really shocked at myself.

Would this kind of lying really affect our mindfulness? I think this is a question that you need to explore for yourself. It may be that, in the moment, it doesn't seem to make much difference. But casual lying over a period inevitably leads to some degree of mistrust. Have a think about people that you know well. Who do you trust to always tell the truth? Who do you trust less? Mistrust leads to disconnection, which inevitably makes mindfulness harder. Ultimately, I think that being mindful is about seeing reality as it really is – without any distortions. Isn't that the essence of truth?

REFRAINING FROM INTOXICANTS

It's really, really difficult to be mindful when you are drunk. As much as we like to have a drink in our culture, I think we have to accept that drinking alcohol puts an obstacle in our path when it comes to being clear-sighted. So, does that mean you have to give up drinking to be truly mindful? This question causes a lot of trouble to Western Buddhists. Most Buddhists I know do have an alcoholic drink from time to time. We live in a culture where drinking is a social custom. Refraining from drinking, especially at social occasions, can make you feel isolated and make other people uncomfortable.

I used to drink a lot. In my late teens and early twenties, I was probably drinking between five and ten units a day. But when I was trying to conceive my first child, I gave up drinking entirely. I was still going out to the pub with my friends, but for nine whole months, I just drank orange juice or tonic water without the gin. It was quite a revelation. I found that I could enjoy myself just as much as my tipsy friends, and it was very pleasant to wake up in the morning without a hangover. I was so happy to be pregnant, that giving up drinking didn't feel like a restriction. (Refraining from my favourite cheese and soft-boiled eggs was another story!) Although I started drinking alcohol again after the birth, as a parent I have less opportunity to spend time in the pub. But I haven't just cut down on alcohol for practical reasons: as my commitment to my meditation practice has increased, my alcohol intake has dwindled to a minimal level.

Another aspect to consider is how does alcohol affect our ability to parent? This question also applies to the use of recreational drugs. I have seen parents who, after a couple of drinks, or perhaps having smoked a joint, are not able or willing to fully engage with their children. Sometimes that's OK, because we do need to have moments of relaxation. But sometimes it can go too far. Once, in a scene that pulled on my heartstrings, I saw the disappointment and confusion of a nine-month-old baby

TIP: Drinking with awareness

If we are open to working with the precepts, then I think a wise course of action is to start by simply becoming more aware of how we drink, and what effect it has on our minds. It will probably become clear that binge drinking does not promote mindfulness! It may be that drinking in more moderation, and with a different approach, makes a significant difference to your state of mind. Abstaining from time to time – and noticing any craving – makes a useful experiment too.

when his father was too drunk to focus on and respond to his smiles. I'm not saying all this to lecture. We all have moments in life when we are not able to parent in the way we want to, and thankfully our children are extraordinarily forgiving. But I think it is worth looking at drinking alcohol and considering – how much is this at odds with what we are trying to do? Or are the positives outweighing the negatives?

I think that if we are going to take the precepts seriously, we need to consider how they apply in the context of our own lives. These are not rules set in stone – if they are to be useful to us, we need to explore them with an open mind. Giving up drinking may have a serious negative impact. As our children get older, we also need to think about what we are modelling to them. It may be that demonstrating how to drink in moderation is an invaluable lesson. Simply shunning alcohol could send the wrong message. In fact, if it feels like a self-inflicted punishment, it's probably not going to be helpful for your state of mind – and a calm unruffled mind is what we are aiming for.

REFINING OUR BEHAVIOUR

As mindfulness deepens, practitioners tend to find that their understanding of the precepts becomes more and more refined. So at first, we might easily forgo stealing from a shop, for example. But as we cultivate an increased awareness of our actions we start to feel uncomfortable about smaller transgressions.

In the case of the first precept, for example, a commitment not to kill a human being is fairly easy for most. However, in time you may come to feel less happy about the idea of other people killing – perhaps in wars. You may come to extend this idea to killing animals, including pests such as slugs and flies. Although most Buddhists I know are not vegetarian, you may decide to eat less meat. Some people find that the first precept comes to include any kind of harm that causes fear and pain to living creatures. You may even consider what actions cause harm to yourself, such as unhealthy eating.

I'm a keen recycler and I had a habit of reusing unfranked stamps that came through the post. After a while I became more conscious that this amounted to stealing from the post office. I started to feel guilty when peeling them off the envelope. I still carried on doing it for a while, until I realized that for the sake of a few pence, I was inviting guilt in and causing disturbance to my mind. Was it worth it? From then on I chucked the tempting envelopes straight in the wheelie bin outside, and tried to celebrate the opportunity to be skilful.

WHAT DO I MEAN BY SKILFUL?

The term *skilful* comes up quite a lot in Buddhist teaching. To put it simply, Buddhism pretty much divides up all actions, thoughts and speech into two camps: either skilful or unskilful. Buddhists believe that skilful actions help us to move closer toward happiness and enlightenment, and unskilful ones create obstacles.

I find the term really useful, which is why I'm using it here. We could say 'ethical' or 'unethical', but I think these terms are often too strong, and too loaded with judgement. For example, let's say you interrupt someone while they are talking – we wouldn't tend to describe this as 'unethical', but I think it is clear that it is slightly unskilful behaviour. We could talk about actions being helpful or unhelpful, but I like the way skilful implies a degree of effort.

GENEROSITY AS A PRACTICE

I've just talked a lot about refraining from unskilful behaviour, as a means to protect our mindfulness practice. But what about developing positive behaviours? Buddhism places a very high value on the practice of generosity. In the West we have a tendency to think of this type of quality as something that is fixed: 'Joe is so generous.' 'My granddad is really tight-fisted.' But, as we keep on finding, with both mindfulness and the qualities of boundless love (see Chapter 4), all these qualities can be cultivated and increased. Think of Scrooge in *A Christmas Carol*. All we have to do is be open to the idea in the first place, and then to keep on practising it.

IS GENEROSITY REALLY SUCH A GOOD THING?

We all know in theory that generosity is 'a good thing'. However, to what extent do we really embrace that idea? I know that I struggle with it. When I think about generosity I start to get a bit panicky: but if I'm more generous, won't I be worse off? After all, Scrooge had lots of money he didn't need. I'd love to be more generous, but I can't afford it.

Part of the problem is that we are bombarded with requests for money from all sides, to the extent that we are left with the impression that generosity is *only measured in money*. In fact, that is a really limited way of looking at it. I must admit that I sometimes feel a bit ambivalent about giving money to charity. When I looked at this more closely I realized it's because the fundraisers are often not directly connected to the cause. Paid charity workers collecting on the street don't always seem very genuine. Sometimes we can even feel like we've been cheated out of our money – this isn't the type of generosity we want to cultivate; it may be giving money, but it's not generosity.

In many cases, much of the money donated to charity is going toward paying staff salaries. Now I don't have a problem with this in itself as of course it's necessary for charities to pay their staff. But what this means in effect, is that we are *paying somebody else to do the charity work for us*. When we give money to a homeless charity, for example, that's not the same as working a shift in a soup kitchen, or buying a coffee for a homeless person in town. It's as if we are buying our way out of the inconvenience of helping other people ourselves. And what happens then is that we don't get the same feedback and reward that comes with actually doing the charitable work itself.

TIP: Giving and charity

Charities do invaluable work in bringing good causes to our attention. But if we are focusing on developing a generous attitude within ourselves, often it is best to look for opportunities to be generous closer to home. We can look out for small ways to be helpful as we go about our business. Holding the door open for someone, giving way in traffic, helping someone carry their shopping, holding a baby for another parent while they do a chore, signing a petition, baking someone a cake ... there are countless ways for us to practise generosity. We may also consider making a bigger commitment by seeking out a volunteering opportunity.

I am not saying that we should stop giving money to charities. But rather this is not *the only way* to practise generosity. In fact, it might be quite hard to practise generosity in this way at first. Sometimes, giving money to charity really does come from generosity. An acquaintance of mine recently raised funds to provide survival essentials for refugees arriving in Lesvos. I had already been moved by the plight of the refugees, but something had held me back from donating. When I saw her crowd funding appeal, I was happy to donate what for me was a significant amount. Rather than thinking of her as a middleman in the charity process, I felt that I was giving to *her* to enable her to pursue her heart mission. This felt good.

HOW GENEROSITY MAKES US FEEL

If someone asks me for money on the street, I am inclined to feel defensive. But at the same time, I can feel that this reaction makes me feel diminished and weaker. I feel slightly ashamed of myself. I have to learn how to overcome this, both for my own benefit, and so that I don't pass this resistance on to my children.

What often holds me back from being generous is a feeling of scarcity. Questions such as,

- Is this the most effective charity?
- Is my money being well spent?
- Do I have time to bake a cake?
- Will my donation be enough?

All these questions are really manifestations of doubt, preventing me from allowing generosity to arise. I start to think of reasons why I shouldn't give my time or money: *I'm in a rush; I already have too many demands; I don't have enough money.* Of course, sometimes those reasons are absolutely legitimate. But when they are our knee-jerk reaction, they can make us feel small and miserly and closed inside. When, on the other hand, we are coming from a base level of open-heartedness, then saying 'No, not this time' doesn't make us feel small and defensive. It's just an honest recognition of the way things are.

In her wonderful book *Loving-kindness: The Revolutionary Art of Happiness*, Sharon Salzberg discusses the cultivation of generosity.[24] She shows us that helping other people makes us feel good. I can recognize that when I am generous with my time and energy, I get a huge satisfaction from that because it makes me feel valued. I just don't like to be put on the spot. Perhaps it is because the request for help or money is almost a challenge to us: *How generous are you, really?* And we may ironically respond to that by giving some excuse as to why it's not reasonable to expect us to help.

ENCOURAGING GENEROSITY IN OUR CHILDREN

Part of my inner resistance to requests for help may be due to the fact that giving was not highly valued in my own upbringing. In the East giving and sharing is a major part of the culture and spiritual practice. It's not emphasized so much in the West. Instead, capitalism has taught us that we should each be able to buy what we need for ourselves. Shining a light on our own attitudes toward giving really helps us to see how best we can encourage this quality in our children. Modelling generosity is a powerful tool. This could be in the way we behave with our children – are we generous with our time and attention? But it can also be in the way we interact with people outside the family. Letting them see us help other people in need, and encouraging them to help too, can foster habits and attitudes for life.

There are many practical ways that we can encourage our children to be more generous.

DE-CLUTTERING THE TOY PILE

Children have many, many toys. They have so many it can actually stifle their ability to play (as we discussed in Chapter 6, see page 76). It can be really tempting to sort through the toys while they are asleep and send a bag off to the charity shop. However, this is missing a great opportunity to encourage them to be generous themselves. But this needs to be approached with a very light touch. Forcing or persuading the children to give away their toys can have the opposite effect. It can make them feel as if their possessions need to be guarded jealously. In such cases, I have to remind myself that the important thing is about cultivating the right attitude, not how many toys we can clear.

One great way to encourage the children to let go of toys is to head out to a swap shop. We have quite a few of these events in my town: they are jumble sales where no money changes hands. I ask the children to gather the toys they don't want, and then we donate them to the swap shop, and pick out a few toys in return. We normally also return with one or two of those we had earmarked to give away. If you don't have a swap shop near you, you could do a similar thing at the charity shop.

TIP: Show by example

Let the children see you sorting through your belongings for donation too. Tell them what you are doing and how the charity shop/jumble sale will benefit. Having them present when you actually hand the goods over to the charity shop can reinforce the point too. (Though be prepared that one or two items might be reclaimed at this point, and don't make a big deal of it.)

Although not quite the same, my daughter became pretty good at de-cluttering her toy pile when she was saving up money to buy a rabbit. She decided to set up a stall outside our house and sold her toys to raise funds. She was of course getting something out of it, in the form of a few pence, but she was also learning to let go and, after the sale, she was quite willing to donate the remainder of the toys to the charity shop. So, in essence, the stall worked as a stepping-stone for her.

My four-year-old still finds it pretty difficult to let go of his possessions. One method I find works fairly well is to take a selection of books (or cars, or cuddlies), for example, and ask him to sort it into three piles – one for keeping, one for throwing, one for giving. This way he is making a positive choice about the books he wants, as well as deciding which to shed. Of course, I would be a lot more ruthless than him, but for the moment I have learnt to respect his decision. With practice, they do get better in time. My seven-year-old recently chose to give away 48 of her 52 soft toys. I had to pull some of them out of the discard pile myself!

GIVING TOYS TO FRIENDS

Well-meaning adults sometimes undermine children's natural generosity. I have often witnessed children spontaneously offering one of their toys to another child, but then a parent steps in and disallows it. Most often this is the parent of the receiving child, who is concerned by the gift. Sometimes they will immediately suggest some kind of swap in return or say that it is only a lend.

TIP: Easy opportunities to practice giving

Another great way for children to experience the positives of giving, without the potential negatives, is to encourage them to hand out gifts such as snacks to other children. Even toddlers are able to offer round a plate of apple slices to their peers at a toddler group. If the child feels that the gift is something to do with them, it can have even more effect. For example, you could get him to hand out slices of his own birthday cake, or the party bags. Similarly you can look for opportunities for children to put money in charity boxes, or give to the homeless or buskers on the street.

Sometimes I've seen it happening the other way round – a parent prevents their own child from giving away a toy. I've even done this myself. ('*Oh no, not that one! You've had that since you were born.*') If you find yourself doing this, try to catch yourself and find out why. Is it because an important relative gave it? Or the toy cost a lot of money? Those factors may be important, but think about what kind of message you are sending to your child. I can think of a couple of occasions when I might query a gift – that would be if I felt another child was pressuring mine to give something, or if I felt that he was likely to regret it later. If so, I would probably just ask: 'Are you sure?' and maybe suggest a different toy.

If my child has offered to share part of the treat he is eating, for example, I would then make sure that he got to choose how much he wanted to give. Otherwise, if I forced him to 'share it fairly', that could interfere with the spirit of giving, and make him feel as if he had got a raw deal.

MAKING GIFTS FOR FRIENDS

Another great way to encourage giving, and also to reduce our entrenched consumerism, is to help our children to make gifts for other people. It doesn't have to be on a special occasion. They could simply bake a batch of fairy cakes for the rest of the family, for example. I have noticed that children will naturally tend to save treats (or a portion of them) for their parents anyway. We can encourage them to expand this circle of generosity by allowing them to create an abundance of good things.

They can also be encouraged to offer their time in the form of services, perhaps helping with chores around the house. Or they may like to do special things for other children, such as teach them a new skill they have learnt or help them in a task.

HELPING CHILDREN SHARE

I often see well-meaning parents urging their children to share toys. Of course, we all want our children to be generous and kind, and we want to be seen to be encouraging those qualities. However, I do think that parents tend to be over-hard on their own children in this respect. For example, I recently saw a three-year-old boy playing with a car at a children's centre. When a younger toddler wandered over and made a grab for the toy, his mother said, 'You can *share* that one, Ollie!' It's no wonder that children find sharing difficult – they come to understand *sharing* to mean: 'passively accepting when another child snatches from you.'

And what exactly do we mean by *sharing*? For a child who is learning how to share, we need to be *much* more explicit about what sharing actually looks like. It's not good enough to just tell two squabbling children that they need to share. They have to be given step-by step instructions. Frankly, I don't think it is very easy to share a toy car. How would two children do that? Would they both put their fingers on it and push it together? Not very likely! In cases like this, it makes a lot more sense to think about turn-taking. Ollie can share the toy car by letting the other toddler have a turn when he is finished. And we may want to encourage him to finish a bit quicker when someone else is waiting.

My rough rule of thumb is that the word *sharing* is for a cake, pieces of apple, the Lego, a *basket* of cars – in short, anything that can be divided up. It also works for really big things like a climbing frame. Some toys, such as a ball, have special rules attached to them; it is quite easy to give clear instructions on sharing a ball. *Turn-taking* is for toys or items that need to be used one at a time, such as a single car, a ride-on toy, a puppet. A ball might fall into this category if a child is playing with it in a certain way. You may be able to encourage your child to finish his turn with it, and then start to share it. Although it may still be hard for him to hand it over to another child, at least he can appreciate that the rules are fair. The problem with forcing children to give up toys when they are not ready is that, in the long term, it makes them *less* inclined to be generous with their possessions. This is especially true if they don't feel they are protected by any rules of conduct. They start to think that they have to guard possessions fiercely.

The question of sharing came up for us very acutely when our children were young, as we began childminding when our own daughter was around 14 months old. At first we presumed that our mindees could play with all the family's toys. After a while, however, it became apparent that our daughter was finding this very difficult. Together, we divided all the toys into upstairs and downstairs. The special ones were kept in her bedroom upstairs. She didn't have to share them if she didn't want to. In fairness to the other children, she was not allowed to play with them in their presence, unless she was willing to share them or let the others have a turn. We applied the same principle to toys the mindees brought from home. If they didn't want to share them, we asked them to keep them safe in their bags. This way, the rules were consistent for all the children: toys that were downstairs were to be played with, and shared fairly; 'ownership' would not have an effect. A similar system of shared toys and a few personal toys can also work among siblings.

HOW GOOD ARE YOU AT SHARING?

Of course, modelling plays a big part. Although we pay a lot of lip service to the notion of sharing, the reality is that our culture has very little respect for it. That's why we live in such self-contained units, each equipped with every possible tool that we could ever need. In virtually every single house in the street, you will find an identical set of kitchen equipment, major appliances, DIY tools, lawn mowers and the list goes on. Some of these items we only use a few times a year.

Being aware of the lack of sharing in our culture can help us find ways to redress the balance. And there are some lovely examples of sharing around. Our neighbour put us on her insurance and let us drive her car for several years. Nowadays there are some great initiatives springing up that promote sharing and community spirit – websites that co-ordinate lift-shares, for example, and community resources where people share equipment and services in their neighbourhoods. (Check page 245 for websites.) These initiatives help us forge connections with our neighbours and provide us with opportunities to practise generosity. They also provide a great model for children.

BEING AN ACTIVE CITIZEN

Being an active citizen is also linked to the concept of generosity. It's also born out of the qualities of boundless love – especially compassion. I think that there is a kind of generosity involved in giving a cause our time, attention or energy. It may seem at first glance that there is not much children can do in the way of citizenship. They are only children, for a start. However, nurturing their innate impulses to be kind to other people and to put things right is one way that we can contribute to a positive world for the future. And, as the children's rights activist, and youngest ever Nobel Peace Prize winner, Malala Yousafzai has shown, children can be powerful agents for change.

Of course, no parent would wish that their child go through the ordeals of Malala Yousafzai, who was shot in the head at age 15 after speaking out against the Taliban. However, we can still help our children to be a force for good in their own way.

We have to be careful, though – children need to be protected from the worst of the news while they are young. If they are going to grow up equipped to deal with the problems of the world, they need to believe that it is essentially 'a good place' for as long as possible. If they become frightened and overwhelmed by the bad in the world at too young an age, they will not be able to confront it. Similarly, they can become desensitized to distressing news stories, and begin not to care. So we have to be really careful about how we filter news to our children.

Having said this, presenting our children with real-life problems, and involving them in ways that we can put them right, is a great way to build their confidence and set them up with the belief that they can make a difference in this world. It will almost certainly influence the way we get involved in activism, too.

When my daughter was three and a half, a mother was told that she had to stop breastfeeding her four-week-old baby in the shoe section of our local Debenhams. A barrage of social media outrage followed, and a breastfeeding sit-in was arranged. I can remember explaining the situation to my daughter. I told her that the shop people didn't like seeing the Mummy feed her baby, and wanted her to stop or move. My daughter was shocked. It was the first time that I had admitted that there was injustice in the world. But I was able to tell her that we could go to the shop and help the staff learn that they had made a mistake. Debenhams, to its credit, immediately retrained all its staff on women's rights, and they invited breastfeeding mums, babies and supporters to a party in their café, where they provided free coffee and cake. Result!

TIP: Finding ways to empower children

Look out for causes or campaigns that you think may capture the interest of your children and help them to come up with ways to support that cause. The issues could be something affecting the local community, or they could be from further afield. Children can raise money through cake stands or asking for sponsorship, or they could write a letter to a company or politician.

This was a particular incident where I was able to link some 'bad news' with something positive that we could do. Some other issues are harder to tackle. For example, I remember when my daughter first learned about children starving in Africa. 'I want to go there and take them some food,' she said simply. I found myself immediately answering, 'It isn't as simple as that . . .' But then I realized that I was letting my own feelings of inadequacy and disempowerment infect her natural impulse to relieve suffering. I was shutting down the urge to help.

With a bit more time to consider and be mindful, I could see that a much more positive response could have been, 'Yes, I'd like to do that too. I don't think I can afford to actually visit there – but shall we try to find some other way to help them get food?'

Even if you don't actually do anything to help, at least you haven't immediately thrown cold water on the impulse. Even better, if you do actually follow through and involve your child in a way to help. Letting our children be our guides is a way we can awaken our own natural kindness and generosity, and start to become more creative about ways in which we can relieve suffering.

Perhaps the very first message that we can give our children is that we need to take responsibility for our *own* actions, and make sure that *we* do not add any more harm to our world. And the first step toward doing that is to become more aware of how we think and act. We can do this by committing to our meditation practice. This leads us to be more mindful of our actions and their significance, and so helps to build a more solid foundation for the larger society. When we take responsibility for ourselves, we are more able to be mindful of the issues facing the community and the world in which we live.

One of the teachings that resonates most with me at the moment is the simple line, 'Peace in oneself, peace in the world.' When there is peace in me, there is more likely to be peace in my family, and I'm more likely to pass on a feeling of peace to anyone I come into contact with. And of course, vice versa – when I am angry or unsettled, that is likely to spread to my family and anyone I meet. So increasingly I feel that cultivating peace in myself is a moral responsibility, not only for my own wellbeing, but also for the greater collective wellbeing of which we all form a part. In the end it's all we can do: look after our own peace, know that it will spread to others we meet, and know that the more peaceful individuals there are around, the better we, and this planet, will all be in the long run.

Ben, dad to Leo, 6

SUMMARY

- *The way we act is intrinsically linked to our state of mind. Ethical behaviour makes it easier for us to be more mindful.*
- *Parenthood can be a natural time to revaluate our ethical behaviour, as we are motivated to provide a good role model. We also want to make the world a better place for our children.*
- *Buddhism offers a framework of rules that moderate behaviour and help support mindfulness. These are: not harming, not stealing, not lying, not committing sexual misconduct, not indulging in intoxicants.*
- *As we become more mindful, we start to refine our ideas about what is, and what is not acceptable behaviour.*
- *Cultivating generosity makes us feel good and helps us to become more connected to other people. There are many ways besides giving money to practise generosity.*

Introducing Mindfulness to Children

Babies and young children live very much in the present moment. When engaged in an activity they are absorbed by it, presumably not distracted by thoughts about the past or future, or by a running commentary. They often approach the world with a delightful freshness, examining objects around them – a spoon, an insect, a crack in the pavement – with curiosity and wonder.

ARE CHILDREN MINDFUL?

These behaviours sound a lot like mindfulness. Mindfulness helps to prevent us adults from getting tangled in thoughts, and allows us to look at our surroundings in a new way, without judgement. It's tempting to describe children as being naturally mindful – I've done this myself. However, on closer inspection, I don't think it's technically true to say that young children have a lot of mindfulness. Mindfulness includes a quality of recollection – of *knowing* that we are here, now, alive and experiencing the world in this way. It is a *presence* of mind. Of course it's difficult to say for certain exactly what is going on in the minds of our children, but I would hazard a guess that they do not often have this broader, more expansive awareness.

Mindfulness helps us to maintain concentration by keeping watch over our minds, and alerts us when our attention shifts. When we are both mindful and concentrated, we can place our attention on the tiny details of life and, just like the children, call up a natural curiosity about them. Thus in the adult mind, the two qualities work in conjunction to aid focus. Young children however, already have a powerful ability to concentrate, simply because their range of interests is so very much smaller. With limited language, they are unable to conceptualize abstract ideas or even, to a large degree, make judgements about what they experience. And their limited understanding of the world means that they simply don't register much of what goes on around them. So they don't need to deal with so many distracting thoughts. It's not so much that children are mindful, it's that mindfulness enables us adults to access that childlike clarity, yet with full awareness of what we are doing.

CHILDREN LACK PERSPECTIVE

Perhaps one of the main differences between adults practising a high degree of mindfulness, and children who are fully absorbed in the present moment, is that we don't tend to see a quality of allowing or acceptance in children. Although they may be happy to allow and accept when events are pleasant or neutral, as soon as there is a perceived threat to their ego, then they will be quick to react. In this way we could say that children have very little equanimity – they take everything personally.

Children's limited understanding of the world is partly to blame for this lack of equanimity. They cannot see how interconnected everything is, and so can't yet see that everything is governed by cause and effect. They are unable to see beyond their own limited circle of vision and experience, so a bump in the pavement that makes them trip can seem like an attack on their sense of self. This is even more so when another child pushes and shoves in the playground.

I think that this tendency to be very caught up in events also indicates a lack of mindfulness. It is very hard for them to find any space from which to observe what is happening – instead they tend to react immediately.

HOW CHILDREN MOVE AWAY FROM THE PRESENT

As children grow, their language increases and they begin to conceptualize much more. Instead of seeing the world as disjointed incidences to be wondered at, they start to make connections, creating a bigger picture, which gets more complex each day. That characteristic fresh-eyed wonder begins to be replaced with notions of familiarity and categorization. They begin to be more absorbed by their inner worlds of fantasy and imagination. Thoughts come hand in hand with language, and their minds – which no longer need to make sense of their immediate surroundings – are more occupied with the past and the future.

As their brains develop and move toward a more adult mind, their ability to raise mindfulness grows, and also their need for it.

In practising mindfulness, I have Alba's wellbeing and happiness in mind because if I'm calmer and more present in myself she can only benefit from that. I hope that witnessing me will encourage her to explore mindfulness practices to help her through her own life.

Gemma, mum to Alba, 8 months

HELPING OUR CHILDREN BE MORE MINDFUL

As they grow older, moments of mindfulness will occur for children spontaneously, but there is also much we (and they) can do to encourage and value this quality.

THE DIFFICULTIES OF TEACHING MEDITATION EXERCISES

There are a number of beautiful books around that provide simple, playful meditation exercises for children (see page 241). Thich Nhat Hanh's *A Handful of Quiet: Happiness in Four Pebbles* uses pebbles to help access the qualities of loving-kindness and other meditations. In *Sitting Still like a Frog*, Eline Snel suggests that children evoke the image of a frog sitting on a lily pad to help them conjure the feeling of focused attention.

I love the ideas in these books. I think they contain many creative accessible ways to introduce some of the concepts of meditation to children. However, I can't speak from experience here; the truth is my children are *extremely resistant* to the idea of me introducing a meditation exercise.

For a long time I felt a vague sense of failure about the fact that I wasn't teaching my children to meditate. I'm a committed meditator myself, I passionately believe in the value of practising, and I'm even *writing a book about meditation for families*. Surely I ought to be more successful at this? However, I've come to realize that even if we believe in the value of meditation, there are many other factors to consider when we think about teaching it. Even if it seems obvious, introducing a regular practice to your children should be handled with great sensitivity and may not actually be the most appropriate action.

RESISTANCE TO LEARNING 'JUST IN CASE'

I'm not sure exactly what it is about meditation that puts my children off. Mostly I think it's because they don't like being told what to do, especially if they can't immediately see the point if it. In fact, it's not just meditation they resist, they rarely co-operate in any activity where they sense I have some kind of teaching agenda. A friend recently told me about 'The Now Game', where each person takes turns to make a comment starting with 'Now ...' (*Now I see a cloud; now I smell dinner; now I can feel my jumper on my skin.*) I liked the way it gently encouraged us to turn the attention to the present and I decided to try it with my four-year-old. However, within seconds he clammed up, obviously self-conscious – perhaps he had detected that I was looking for some kind of 'correct' answer, and the pressure made him resist altogether.

I'm sure that some children are more suggestible than others, and may be easier to guide. However, from chatting with other parents and teachers, I do believe that resistance to being taught by one's parents is a very common theme among children. In fact, there is a growing body of research that shows that children don't learn very effectively when they are taught according to an external curriculum, i.e. one that someone else has set, rather than following their own interests. In his book *What's the Point of School?* Professor Guy Claxton puts it neatly when he says that children like to learn 'just in time' rather than 'just in case'.[25] He argues that learning happens most effectively when children are highly motivated to understand something or acquire a skill, because they need that knowledge or skill *in that moment*, in order to tackle some real problem or activity. So, for example, when a child wants to make an item of clothing for a toy, this is a perfect time to learn how to sew or knit. Or when a child wants to spend her pocket money, this is an opportunity for learning maths with coins and money.

Generally I've found it hasn't worked to suggest directly that they try a formal practice. Introducing practices more informally, as a kind of game, seems to work better. And modelling my own practice – they see that it's important to me, and they feel the sense of calm and quiet it generates.

Guin, MBCP meditation teacher and mum of three

CHECKING OUR OWN INTENTION

Clearly, having a formal meditation practice brings invaluable benefit to adults. It helps top up our reserves of mindfulness, so that we are more able to apply it in day-to-day moments. I'll cover this in more detail in Chapter 12. So it follows that regular meditation practice would also hugely benefit children. However, if children can't feel the immediate benefits of a practice, they may well be resistant. And the benefits can be subtle and hard to detect straight away. That's why so many adults find it difficult to maintain a practice.

I often come across parents who are new to mindfulness asking how they can introduce it to their children. Very often, parents hope that meditation will encourage their children to go to sleep more easily, manage their anger, stay calmer, reduce anxiety, and so on. I think that we need to be really clear about our intention when we set out to teach meditation to children. It is somewhat dangerous to consider meditation to be a kind of remedy that will 'fix' these common childhood problems – all we need to do is teach them to breathe and these problems will magically disappear.

That's not to say that meditation won't help – it certainly could help all these issues. But if we are only presenting mindfulness on a surface level, then it will be hard for our children to access the full depth of the practice. It will also be tempting to measure the success of the meditation by looking at the outcomes. In many ways this is reasonable – of course we want to see some benefits. But if we are always looking toward the outcome, then this can get in the way of the practice.

Sometimes there is another motive at play: we may encourage our children to take up activities and practices that we would like to do ourselves. For example, we might like our children to learn to play the piano, or learn a language, because we never had the chance. With meditation there can be a sense that by teaching it to our children, they might be able to avoid some of the difficulties we ourselves face. This motive is often accompanied by the notion: *it's too late for us.* So instead of working on our own practice, we put our energy into encouraging our children to meditate. If our children then show resistance, or don't seem to be 'doing it right' or taking it seriously enough, then we can end up feeling frustrated and angry.

DEVELOP YOUR OWN PRACTICE

I believe that the very best foundation for teaching meditation to children is to establish a firm practice ourselves. First I think we have an almost moral obligation to take care of our own minds before we start judging and instructing others. If we are struggling with our children's behaviours, then setting out to teach them meditation could have the side effect of reinforcing the notion that our own happiness is dependent on external factors – life would be so much easier if only my daughter would stop having tantrums, go to bed without a fuss, etc. Encouraging our children to meditate may well help, but it is far more important to work on developing our own equanimity (as I discussed in Chapter 4, see page 53). We can't take responsibility for other people's thoughts or actions – not even our children's. Without equanimity, we are likely to feel disempowered and frustrated, especially if meditation doesn't seem to be going the way we'd like.

TIP: Commit to your own practice

When we commit to doing our own work, and do it wholeheartedly, then we are doing the best we can for our children too. Once we have grasped that, then it can be very empowering. Secondly, having a strong understanding and experience of the practice yourself will make you a far more effective teacher.

In the tradition I meditate with, teachers are chosen with great care. Meditators are only deemed ready to teach others once they have developed their own practice over many years and retreats, under the guidance of other teachers, and they have an understanding of how others might develop through study and insight.

Now we may not have the opportunity to spend years meditating before we teach our children, but I do think that we need to teach from a place of experience. The fact is that if you are simply repeating other people's words as an instruction, and cannot really raise the qualities of the meditation yourself, then the words will be empty of meaning. How can you convey understanding if you don't have it yourself? I therefore think we parents need to set our own house in order before we try to help our children to manage theirs.

I don't introduce any kind of meditation practice at home. I think that it's important that children are allowed to discover their own strategies to settle themselves. A flavour of the practice can be inspiring for them but the seeds of that inspiration will bear fruit in their own time and space.

Gwil, meditation teacher and dad to a son, 6, and daughter, 3

SEIZING MOMENTS FOR TEACHING

The great thing about this approach is that once we have established a mindfulness practice ourselves, we will start to find many, many opportunities to teach and demonstrate mindfulness. Reading books, which set out meditation practices for children, can give you ideas to keep up your sleeve for the right moment. However, I think it's wise to approach this with the lightest of touch. We need to let go of any ideas about how children ought to practise, and how often or for how long. Otherwise we are bound to be disappointed and frustrated. But you may find you can lightly incorporate some ideas into rituals and routines that you already have. For example, you could include taking some long breaths at bedtime. Or you could ask your child what it feels like when you give her a back rub. You can draw her attention to her breath as she blow bubbles.

An important way to teach will be to model your own practice. One obvious way to do this may be sitting formally. From the point of view of your actual practice, this is best done away from the children (more on this in Chapter 13, see pages 199–201), but the occasional time when your children stumble across you or interrupt you will provide them with a powerful example. I've noticed that even when my son enters the room with the intention of getting my attention, he will still tiptoe up to me – as if he senses something special in the quietness of the room.

I love the way Andrew says 'Dad's being a Buddha' when he sees me practising. This is very apt because in Zen they say that the *zazen* posture IS enlightenment. When we sit, we are already enlightened, we just need to realize it. I like the idea that he can see it in me.

Gareth, dad to Andrew, 6

We can also demonstrate our informal mindfulness practice, as often as we remember! At first it may feel as if your children are completely oblivious to your heightened awareness, but over time this can be a very powerful influence. As Eluned Gold points out in her essay 'Mindfulness with Children', children soak up the behaviours of those around them and unconsciously use these as templates to guide their own behaviour.[26] If we fly off the handle at every little thing, they will tend to do that too.

My children would encourage me to go and practise, if they thought I needed it. So they must have been able to see the benefits.

Anne, mum to Stephen, 24, Clare, 24, Helen, 23, and Sarah, 20

Informal mindfulness can also be influential in the moment. If we meet difficult situations with reactiveness and heedlessness, then our children will naturally mirror us and the situation will escalate. However, if they sense that we are calm and reflective then this will have the opposite effect. It may not be enough to completely calm them down, but it will probably help somewhat.

Most of us will have had the experience of someone entering a room in a temper and immediately the whole room feels tense. Other people's moods can infect our own (especially if we are not mindful). But this means that our mindfulness itself can be 'catching'.

There is also a place for a small amount of explaining – at the right moment. You can give your children valuable information that they may be able to apply as tools by themselves. However, this needs to be done very carefully, to avoid our children dismissing our instruction as 'boring adult talk'. Once, when my daughter was about three, she was screaming in an uncontrollable tantrum. I suggested that she try breathing, as that might help her find space and calm down a little. As far as I knew, she completely ignored me. She carried on screaming. However, about a year later, we were talking about crying, and she said casually, 'If I don't want to cry, I just breathe instead.' I was staggered. Unbeknownst to me she had obviously taken on board my suggestion and worked out how to use it for herself.

We can also encourage mindfulness through skilful listening. In Chapter 4 (see pages 47–48) I discussed how we can cultivate and express our own compassion by careful listening when our child is in pain – without rushing in to solve the problem. This also provides an opportunity for our children to develop mindfulness along with compassion. By not crowding out their thoughts with remedies and solutions, we give them time and space to notice what's going on inside their bodies and minds. Sometimes, it's appropriate to draw their attention inward – *How did that make you feel? What do you think about that?* This helps them understand that it's useful to take notice of what is going on inside our minds and bodies, and also it gives them a language and framework for talking and thinking about these issues.

Sometimes we may find a teaching opportunity crop up during casual conversation. My daughter recently remarked that she can't stop reading all the words around her – on labels, food packaging, etc. It was very tempting to jump in with my superior knowledge and say something like – *Oh that's because the mind wants to be stimulated* – or something equally boring. But eventually I realized that a more useful response was to encourage her to be curious about the way her mind works. 'Why do you think it does that? How do you feel after you keep reading the same word over and over?'

MEDITATION PRACTICE:
Quiet moments

We can build quiet moments into our day to provide opportunities for mindfulness. Rituals such as lighting a candle before dinner can give us time to pause and recall the present moment. We don't need to make a big deal of it. Ideally, we can act and speak authentically. (*'I read about lighting a candle in a book, and I thought it might be a nice way to mark the beginning of the meal. Would you like to hold the match?'*) If your children think you are playing some kind of a part, they will call you up on it.

Chanting or listening to chants together is another accessible way to meditate in itself. This type of meditation is highly valued in the East, but hasn't been embraced by the secular mindfulness movement in the same way as sitting practice has. If you find the unfamiliarity of the chants themselves difficult, you could simply spend time singing familiar songs together.

Children are much more likely to understand the value of meditation if they can approach it playfully, and on their own terms. And, actually, if we think about it, that's how we adults learn best too! Our own beliefs about meditation – for example, how we ought to practise it, and what 'success' looks like – may be holding us back in our own practice. If we are setting out to 'teach' meditation, we need to be careful that we don't pass on those beliefs to our children too.

WHEN CHILDREN WANT TO LEARN FOR THEMSELVES

As children get a little older, and they can understand the benefits, they may become more receptive to the idea of learning meditation as an actual practice. However, you may still find that you are not their best teacher! Some parents get around this by listening to audio recordings with their children, or encouraging them to listen by themselves. That way the teaching voice comes from someone else. There are countless meditations available to listen to on the Internet (See Appendix II, pages 244–245 for some websites.)

Many schools are now cottoning on to the benefits of mindfulness and programmes are currently being piloted across the country. So it may be that your child will learn formal meditation at school. I'm very interested to see how this will develop. Just like with parents teaching children, it seems to me equally important that the right people are teaching meditation in schools for the right reasons. You may be asked to encourage your child at home with their meditation practice – in which case you'll need to investigate carefully whether you think it is being taught skilfully, and how you might support that.

My husband and I meditate with a tradition that offers family retreats, so I am hoping that in time my children will take up the opportunity to meditate with teachers at the retreat centre, and perhaps even go on their own young people's retreat in the future.

FINDING THE MIDDLE WAY

I was discussing the subject of teaching children to meditate with one of my teachers (himself a father of three boys) and he told me a story. He had been visiting a Buddhist temple and got into a discussion with a monk he knew there. The monk asked him whether he taught his children meditation. My teacher said that he did not, but they knew where to find him if they wanted to learn. The monk gently admonished him saying, 'That's not the middle way!'

My teacher thought it was very interesting that what to him seemed a liberal and fair approach of letting his children decide for themselves if they wanted to learn meditation, was, to the monk, an *extreme* way of raising children. He felt that the middle way would be encouraging meditation without being strict and rigid about it.

I think that the middle way is to teach mindfulness whenever it is helpful. To do that we need to recognize when a direct approach would be unhelpful and think creatively about opportunities for teaching. Much teaching can be done through modelling, supported by timely, well-chosen suggestions. As children grow older, we may be able to advocate meditation more strongly. But, ultimately, if they are going to get something out of it, they will have to come to the practice themselves – it's not something you can impose on them.

SUMMARY

- *Young children live in the present, though they don't technically have a lot of mindfulness.*
- *Although it may seem to make sense, it can be hard for parents (especially) to teach meditation exercises to their children, as they may be resistant.*
- *We need to firmly establish our own practice before we focus on teaching meditation to our children.*
- *Teaching through modelling of formal and informal practice can be very powerful. Children can 'catch' our mindfulness.*

- *When the right moments present themselves, we can encourage children to look inward.*
- *When children want to learn for themselves, it may be your job to help them find a teacher, rather than teach them yourself.*

12

Formal Meditation

In the last chapter, I talked a lot about the importance of developing our own practice in order to be the best guides to our children. It is possible to simply practise meditation just whenever we remember, as we go about our day, as I described in Chapter 2 (see pages 18– 19). However, there are specific benefits for setting aside regular periods for formal meditation.

The trouble with trying to maintain a practice without formal meditation is that we have nothing to anchor us to it when life gets distracting and so we start to forget to be mindful. Regular formal meditation can be a way of rooting the practice into our lives. When we sit for a formal practice, we are making a commitment to be mindful for that period. I like to think of it as 'meditating in laboratory conditions'. When we dedicate specific time to meditating, we can set it up so that there will be minimal external distractions. This, in theory, makes it easier to meditate, as you can be more focused. A calm, quiet space makes it easier for us to develop concentration, and the lack of activity serves as a reminder for us to keep calling up mindfulness. (In reality, however, your thoughts may be just as, if not more, distracting than external factors!)

Another good reason to set aside a specific time is that you are much more likely to stay committed to the meditation during that time. You are also likely to meditate for longer, which gives your brain a chance to make more neurons. (Research has found that the brain actually grows during meditation![27]) You may be able to go deeper into the meditation and find new levels of calm and awareness. This 'tops you up' with mindfulness and gives you resources to draw on until your next meditation session.

The relationship between formal meditation and the quality of the mind during daily life is extremely interesting. It is clear that each feeds off and affects the other. Once you have established a regular practice, it is quite easy to see how the concentrated periods of mindfulness start to infuse the whole day, making you more able to maintain calm and spaciousness in everyday circumstances. Equally, we start to find that the way we act in the day affects our practice. If we have lost our temper, or are particularly worried or anxious about a situation, for example, then this tension will linger in the mind and manifest itself in some way during the practice.

HOW OFTEN SHOULD I PRACTISE?

Any amount of formal meditation you can do will have a positive impact on your overall quality of mind. Even if you only manage to sit quietly once a week, or even once a month, then this contact will go some way toward keeping you in touch with a deeper level of awareness. However, it is also true to say that meditating more regularly will help build up a kind of momentum, which cannot really be created if you only sit sporadically.

Different traditions and schools of thought may suggest different frequencies of formal meditation. The tradition I practise with advises a single daily practice of around 30–40 minutes. Other schools recommend meditating twice a day, perhaps for a shorter period. Different frequencies and lengths of sits may reflect the type of meditation taught. I have heard it said that a single longer period may help develop a calm, concentrated mind, while more frequent shorter periods may favour mindfulness with a more flexible mind.

There seems to be a consensus that a daily (or near-daily) practice is ideal for helping to raise momentum. A daily practice becomes a kind of thread to work with, rather than just isolated periods of awareness and calm. This can seem like a very big commitment – especially if you are a parent. You may feel you simply don't have this amount of time to spare. And at certain times in our lives this will literally be the case. However, if you are really committed to the idea of establishing a regular practice, then there is normally *something* you can do to carve out some time for yourself. Though it will probably take a fair bit of juggling and reprioritizing. I'll talk about the practicalities of doing this in Chapter 13.

If something goes wrong and I don't get my usual practice time I do my best to still practise but maybe for just five or 10 minutes. Generally whatever happens there are five minutes to spare, and that five minutes of formal practice could change the way the rest of the day unfolds.
Guin, MBCP meditation teacher and mum of three

You may actually find that committing to meditating every day is actually much easier than sitting once or twice a week, as it becomes a habit you no longer need to think about, much in the same way that you might take a shower or brush your teeth.

Don't be too 'hard line' about formal practice because parenting itself is a practice. If you genuinely cannot practise without it inconveniencing someone else, just practise mindfulness in everyday tasks and make that your practice for the day. However, if you can find the time I'd recommend it.
Deborah, meditation teacher and mum to Jesse, 20, and Rowan, 17

SO WHAT IS A FORMAL MEDITATION?

The first thing I need to say is that I don't believe meditation is best learned from a book. (Or, for that matter, from the Internet, an app or an audio device.) The most effective way to learn meditation is from a teacher in a real-life class. A good teacher will be able to guide you through the different stages of the meditation – introducing each one at the right time for your level – and answer your questions as they arise. They (along with your fellow meditators) will model their own practice and provide structure, support and encouragement in yours. I will talk in much greater depth about the role of teachers and classes in Chapter 14.

Having said that, I think it is useful to have a clear idea of what is meant by formal meditation practice, especially if you are new to mindfulness. So for that reason, I am going to include instructions for two meditation practices here, one drawn from a Buddhist tradition and another from a secular tradition.

I also know that some of you will find it hard to access a meditation class (again I'll talk more about that in Chapter 14) or you may not yet be ready to make that kind of commitment. If that's the case, you may like to experiment with these exercises here on your own. That's perfectly fine. A book can never be a substitute for a real-life teacher, but it may help you get started.

CHOOSING THE RIGHT MEDITATION

There are many different organizations offering meditation and mindfulness courses. In the back of the book, you'll find a list of some of these. I don't recommend any one particular method over another. All meditation practices help you cultivate positive mental qualities. When choosing a type of meditation, it may be more important to consider other factors such as the experience and integrity of the teacher, the availability of the class and the theoretical framework that supports the meditation – for example, whether it is set in a spiritual dimension or a psychological one.

MINDFULNESS OF BREATHING

Although we may not realize it, at any one moment our minds are engaged with a single object (e.g. a feeling, or a thought or sensation) and we often switch rapidly between two or more objects. It's not possible for the mind to have no object at all. This is also true during meditation. Sometimes people think meditation is about 'clearing the mind' or 'thinking of nothing', but actually these wouldn't be very helpful instructions.

There are many different ways of meditating, but perhaps the most widely practised of all is mindfulness of breathing. This is when we set out to take the breath as the object that the mind focuses on. The breath is an extremely good object of meditation as it is always present, and yet each breath itself is unique. The breath is said to be perfect for beginners due to its simplicity and because it is suitable for all types of people. However, it is not just for beginners: the most advanced levels of meditation can be reached through breath meditation.

There are different ways to use the breath as an object of meditation, but most practices (at least at first) involve gently turning the mind to the breath in some specific way. Returning to a predetermined object helps to anchor the mind and helps it to settle down.

FINDING THE RIGHT POSTURE

Although formal meditation can be done while sitting, standing, lying or walking, the sitting posture is probably the easiest and best to start with. Correct posture is given a lot of emphasis in Buddhist traditions, while secular mindfulness schools are sometimes more relaxed about it.

In the tradition I meditate with, a lot of care is taken over the posture. In common with most Buddhist traditions, meditators are advised to keep a firm base on the ground, and to sit upright with a straight spine. The cross-legged position is very stable and commonly adopted. Sitting with just the bottom on a firm cushion raises it off the ground, and allows the knees to move downward until they touch the floor. The feet can be in lotus or half-lotus (where either both or one foot rests on the opposite thigh) or they can rest one in front of each other on the floor. (Actually crossing the legs in the way that children naturally sit can constrict the blood flow.) This posture provides a really solid and steady base.

Alternatively, you can use a specifically designed stool. This also raises the pelvis and enables you to kneel on the ground. If you find it too difficult to bend your knees, you can meditate sitting upright on a chair, with your feet firmly placed on the floor. It is

best for the back to be self-supporting, however, and not leaning against the back of the chair.

There are two main reasons for taking care over your posture. The first is that a well-grounded, balanced posture should be very comfortable, and will allow you to sit for a length of time without needing to shift position (and so creating distraction). That said, most beginners find that they encounter some discomfort sitting at first, though this does tend to abate as the body gets used to settling into position. The second reason is that establishing and maintaining an alert posture goes hand in hand with establishing and maintaining an alert mind. They work in partnership together, each supporting the other.

MEDITATION PRACTICE:
Breathing to quiet the mind and body to realize joy

Thich Nhat Hanh is one of the best-known teachers of mindfulness in the West. He is a Buddhist monk originally from Vietnam. He established the Order of Interbeing 50 years ago and has set up a number of international centres, including Plum Village, a monastery in the South of France. He's one of my favourite writers and I had the good fortune to see him give a talk in London a few years ago.

This meditation is taken from Thich Nhat Hanh's *The Miracle of Mindfulness*.

'Sit in the full or half lotus position. Half smile. Follow your breath. When your mind and body are quiet, continue to inhale and exhale very lightly, mindful that, "I am breathing in and making the breath-body light and peaceful." Continue for three breaths, giving rise to the thought in mindfulness, "I am breathing in and making my entire body light and peaceful and joyous." Continue for three breaths and in mindfulness give rise to the thought, "I am breathing in while my body and mind are peace and joy."

'Maintain this thought in mindfulness for 5–30 minutes, or for an hour, according to your ability and the time available. The beginning and end of the practice should be relaxed and gentle. When you want to stop, gently massage your eyes and face with your two hands and then massage the muscles in your legs before returning to a normal sitting position. Wait a moment before standing up.'[28]

MEDITATION PRACTICE:
Mindfulness of breathing – sitting

In *The Mindful Way Through Depression*, Williams, Teasdale, Segal and Kabat–Zinn offer a more detailed meditation practice:

Settling

Settle into a comfortable sitting position. Gently close your eyes if that feels comfortable. If not, let your gaze fall unfocused on the floor four or five feet in front of you.

Bringing awareness to the body

Bring your awareness to the level of physical sensation by focusing your attention on the sensations of touch and pressure in your body where it makes contact with the floor and with whatever you are sitting on. Spend a minute or two exploring these sensations.

Focusing on the sensations of breathing

Now bring your awareness to the changing patterns of physical sensations in the belly as the breath moves in and out of the body.

Focus your awareness on the mild sensations of stretching, as the abdominal wall gently expands with each in-breath and on the sensations of gentle release as the abdominal wall deflates with each out-breath. As best you can, stay in touch with the changing physical sensations for the full duration of the in-breath and of the out-breath, perhaps noticing the slight pauses between an in-breath and the next out-breath; and between an out-breath and the next in-breath. As an alternative, focus on a place in the body where you find the sensations of the breath most vivid and distinct.

There is no need to try to control your breathing in any way – simply let your body breathe by itself. As best you can, also bring this attitude of *allowing* to the rest of your experience – there is nothing that needs to be fixed, and no particular state to be achieved. As best you can, simply surrender to your experience as it is without requiring that it be any different.

Working with the mind when it wanders

Sooner or later (usually sooner), the mind will wander away from the focus on the breath sensations in the belly, getting caught up in thoughts, planning or daydreams, or just aimlessly drifting about. Whatever comes up, whatever the mind is pulled to or absorbed by, is perfectly OK. This wandering and getting absorbed in things is simply what minds do; it is not a mistake or a failure. When you notice that your awareness is no longer focused on the breath, you might want to congratulate yourself because you've already come back enough to know it. You are, once more, aware of your experience. You might like to briefly acknowledge where the mind has been (noting what is on your mind and perhaps making a light mental note: 'thinking, thinking' or 'planning, planning'). Then, gently escorting your attention back to the breath sensations in the belly, as you bring awareness to the feeling of *this* in-breath or *this* out-breath, whichever is here as you return.

However often you notice that the mind has wandered (and this will quite likely happen over and over again), each time take note of where the mind has been, then gently escort your attention back to the breath and simply resume attending to the changing pattern of physical sensations that come with each in-breath and with each out-breath.

As best you can, bring a quality of kindness to your awareness, perhaps seeing the repeated wanderings of the mind as opportunities to cultivate greater patience and acceptance within yourself and some compassion toward your experience.

Continue with the practice for 10 minutes, or longer if you wish, perhaps reminding yourself from time to time that the intention is simply to be aware of your experience moment by moment, as best you can, using the breath as an anchor to gently reconnect with the here and now each time that you notice that the mind has wandered off and is no longer in touch with the abdomen, in touch with this very breath in this very moment.[29]

SUMMARY

- *Sitting regularly for formal meditation is an excellent way to develop your practice. Committing to this focused period of time gives you great resources to draw from throughout the day.*
- *Any amount of formal meditation will have a positive impact, but establishing a daily or near-daily practice will build momentum. Sometimes it's easier to maintain a daily habit rather than finding times as and when.*
- *Meditation is best learned from a teacher in a class.*
- *There are lots of different types of meditation. The most commonly practised is mindfulness of breathing. It is suitable for all types of people, at all stages of experience.*
- *A straight, balanced sitting posture enables you to sit for a length of time and helps to keep the mind alert.*

13

Making Time for Formal Meditation

So you have tried sitting in formal meditation and you are ready to establish a regular daily 'sit'. Or perhaps you have already been meditating for a while, in your pre-family existence. Now it's time to think about how to incorporate meditation into your daily routine.

ESTABLISHING A DAILY PRACTICE IN THE FAMILY HOME

Meditating in ideal conditions looks something like this:

I wake up and switch off the alarm before it even starts to ring. I rise and get dressed. I go to the usual place I meditate: a tidy, uncluttered room. My cushion is stored neatly in its usual place, and I take it out and place it in my normal sitting spot. It is in a clear area with space all around. I light a candle on the table in front of me and then move back into my sitting posture. I breathe, and take a moment to ground myself. There is minimal background noise – I can just make out a ticking clock and the low hum of the fridge in the distance. I close my eyes. I know that I will not be disturbed for the next half an hour. My phone is turned off and no one will come into the room. The whole house is quiet. I begin to meditate.

Meditating in my family is more like this:

I wake up early, sandwiched between my sleeping husband and son, who has snuck into our bed in the night. I try to slide myself out of the bed without disturbing the duvet, but it flickers against his face and his eyes snap open. 'Mum, can we get up now?' he asks.

We go downstairs and I start to make the breakfast. There is a torrent of requests:

'Can I have a lolly for breakfast?'

'Can I watch something?'

'Can you read this?'

'Mum!' My daughter has woken up and is shouting from her bedroom, 'Come upstairs!'

At last my husband has finished his shower and he comes into the kitchen.

'Is it OK if I go and meditate?' I ask, once everyone is eating.

Upstairs, I go back into our room. A mess of clothes and books, and a half-unpacked suitcase from last weekend, make it hard to navigate. The only floor space is directly in front of the door. I look for my meditation cushion. It's not there. Eventually I find it outside in the tree house. It's a bit damp and I have to brush off a woodlouse. Back in our room, I throw some clothes onto the bed to make space to sit cross-legged. I want to light a candle but I can't find the lighter. I close my eyes. I can hear one of the children singing a song; and The Octonauts' theme tune is playing. I start to observe my breath. The door opens behind me.

'Mum?' my son whispers. I keep my eyes closed. 'Mum?' I can feel his lips against my ear. He walks round in front of me and prises open my eyelids. When he is sure I am looking at him he says, 'Can I have a lolly?'

'Can you go and ask Dad, please? I'm meditating.'

I close my eyes again and try to observe my breath. My son lifts up my arm and sits on my knee.

WORKING WITH 'ADVERSE CONDITIONS' MEDITATION

I like to think of the above type of meditation as an 'adverse conditions meditation'. Some people might think that meditating like this is utterly hopeless. I sometimes feel like that. It's not easy to establish a daily sitting practice when the house is in a mess and the children think you are on call, and their noise follows you into the room, even if *they* don't. If you are getting distracted by the noise of your children, or being interrupted every single time you sit, then it can easily feel like you 'are not doing it properly'. It can even leave you feeling frustrated and annoyed, which is exactly the opposite of what you are aiming for.

But the point about meditation is that, although we may try to set up the best conditions we can, at the end of the day, we have to work with what there is. And that 'what' may well be your son trying to prise open your eyes.

Over the next couple of pages I'll go through some practical suggestions for establishing better conditions for a daily sit. I'll also explore the way we think about 'adverse conditions' meditation and consider how we can make it work better for us.

FINDING THE RIGHT TIME

Finding time for formal meditation can be difficult for anyone. But finding time to sit when you have one or more children can sometimes feel impossible. Planning in advance, and setting aside regular time can help.

MEDITATING FIRST THING

A lot of meditation teachers recommend sitting for formal meditation as soon as you wake up. There are good reasons for this – on the practical side, you can just set the alarm clock 30 minutes earlier and then meditate before starting on the usual routines of the morning. This can make it easier to find time to meditate, as you don't have to 'squeeze' the practice in between two other activities. Early morning tends to be a quiet period – the phone is unlikely to ring, traffic noise is less, your partner may be sleeping, etc. I'm also told that another reason for meditating upon waking is that the mind has not yet filled up with the clutter of thoughts to do with the day ahead. I say I've been told this – the truth of the matter is that I have almost *never* managed to meditate first thing, so I can't speak from experience. (The only time I've been able to do this is on retreat – see Chapter 15 for more on this.)

If your children consistently sleep in their own beds, until a regular time, then 'first thing' meditation may well be a good option. It doesn't work for me. My children seem to have a very strong need to 'check in' with me the moment they wake up.

Of course, with a bit of thought, it might be possible for me to reorganize our household morning routine to allow for my husband to take over the early morning childcare. However, I don't think this is necessary: it's not that important to meditate first thing. For us, it makes more sense to find a time in the day that is less intense.

DURING NAPTIME

When I had just one child, who still had naps, I liked to use this time to meditate. Although it was right in the middle of the day, I found it very conducive. There was a consistency about it that helped establish the practice. I also felt in sync with my daughter's natural rhythms: both of us were using the time to rest and replenish ourselves, ready for the afternoon. Her sleep pattern, like most young people, meant that she would either sleep for around 45 minutes, or 1.5 hours. The first stretch of deep sleep allowed me a comfortable amount of time to meditate, and if she slept for a second cycle, then I could do some chores as well.

MEDITATING WHILE YOUR CHILDREN ARE FALLING ASLEEP

Before I joined a meditation class and learnt a specific practice, I had been meditating intuitively as I put my daughter to bed. As a baby, she found it very tricky to fall asleep (sometimes taking an hour or two) and I found that lying beside her, allowing my breath to lengthen and letting my body become very relaxed, eventually seemed to send her strong cues to do the same. While I did this I concentrated on a long relaxed breath, and I'm sure that I derived a lot of benefit from this. I also remember it as a really lovely time for me to *be* with my daughter – staying with my breath – and hers – helped me to enjoy the process rather than feeling frustrated. Once I had started meditating more formally I tried to practise during this time. However, I found it very hard to maintain concentration while lying down. I also found that I was too distracted by what my daughter was doing, to consistently place my attention on something else.

If your child likes you to stay in the room as a reassuring presence, but does not need to be in physical contact, then this may be a suitable option. However, I don't think that your child's bedtime is an ideal time for formal meditation. We can think of the transition from wakefulness to slumber as a kind of journey – from alertness, through fidgeting, to drowsiness and finally to sleep. Being present with them, and helping them along this journey, is a lovely and valuable experience – it can be one of the most precious memories of parenthood (and it's an excellent time for mindfulness – which I explored in more detail in Chapter 5, see pages 67–69). However, your own formal meditation is also a journey, and if you bind it too closely to your child's bedtime journey, you will be unable to explore where your mind can go by itself.

MEDITATING WHILE YOUR CHILDREN ARE ELSEWHERE

If there is a period of time in the week when your child (or children) is/are being looked after by someone else, then this is a great time to meditate. I think many parents feel too guilty to meditate during this time, as they feel that they ought to be doing something 'more productive' like housework or paid work. Don't feel guilty for prioritizing meditation. Skimping on your own needs is actually a false economy. When you feel relaxed and replenished you will be able to use your time more efficiently. Your family will benefit much more from having a calm, engaged parent than a harassed one who has completed the laundry. Of course, it's unlikely you'll have this kind of opportunity every day in the week, but feel free to seize it when it arises.

I have had to be more organized about when I meditate alone. I put aside time to meditate when my son is spending time with his dad or with his childminder.

Kate, mum to Zach, 2½

ASKING YOUR PARTNER TO LOOK AFTER THE CHILDREN

Unless my husband is away or working to a tight deadline, then we normally manage to find time to meditate by taking turns to look after the children. We often find that we need to tinker with the breakfast routine to accommodate everyone's needs. My husband started practising daily last year, so now we have a reciprocal arrangement whereby he goes first, while I get breakfast for myself and the kids, then I go. It can feel strange to prioritize meditation like this, especially so, I think, if it's just you meditating. It's one thing carving time out of your own schedule for meditation, it's another thing to ask someone else to carve time out of *their* schedule to support *your* practice.

But I do think this is worth considering. Although it can feel selfish to demand such a considerable amount of 'me time', in fact you are doing a great job of modelling self-respect. And the benefits to your family are very real and tangible. The fact that others have had to make sacrifices to allow you to meditate can also help you stay committed to the practice – though this may work in different ways for different people.

Now my children are older it is easy to find time; when they were younger I asked my husband to look after them in order to practise.

Deborah, meditation teacher and mum to Jesse, 20, and Rowan, 17

MEDITATING ONCE THE KIDS ARE IN BED

After bedtime is that golden – somewhat mythical – period that we can find ourselves fantasizing about through the day. I tend to compile a list of jobs that I want to get done once the kids are asleep. It's the time for us to reconnect with our partners, eat supper, phone extended family, catch up on some TV, send a few emails . . . the list goes on. In reality, I often find that I'm so exhausted that I just fall asleep while putting my son to bed, and wake up at one in the morning fully dressed without having brushed my teeth. I find it difficult to meditate in the evenings, as I am either too tired, or time feels so short that I simply must do some other things first. Then before I know it, it's 11.30 and I have to go to bed. For many people, however, evening will be the obvious choice for meditation.

It's difficult! But my goal is to practise in the evening when the children have gone to bed.

Jan, mum to Josia, 8, and Hannah, 5

CONSISTENCY VS. FLEXIBILITY

Finding a regular slot to meditate each day undoubtedly helps establish a daily practice. It becomes a habit that we don't need to make a special effort to sustain. It also takes the headache out of working out how to fit in a sit. However, we shouldn't worry if there needs to be more flexibility. Try to pull in some consistency where you can. For example, on your workdays you may meditate during your lunch break, while on other days you meditate after the kids are in bed.

Another way to be consistent when things seem to be chaotic is to have a back-up plan. So, let's say your normal routine is that your partner covers you for a breakfast meditation, but this morning there has been slippage and you can't fit it in. In that case you can revert to plan B – meditating during your child's nap.

TIP: Making use of rituals

Many people find that adding rituals to the beginning of their practice helps the mind to get ready. What do I mean by that? A ritual can be anything that you regularly do before you meditate. Classic examples of rituals are lighting a candle or incense, or even just sitting on a particular cushion. In Buddhist cultures, meditators may chant or bow to a Buddha image. When I first started meditating, I thought that all that kind of stuff was unnecessary trappings and I didn't want anything to do with it. I later found out that rituals actually help a lot. Association is a very powerful tool, so if we regularly perform an action before meditating, just doing that action again can trigger a state of readiness in the mind. Your ritual doesn't have to be anything remotely Eastern or New Age, if that feels uncomfortable. One of my rituals is that I wind my clock before I sit.

I think that rituals are especially useful if other aspects of your practice are less consistent. For example, if you have to snatch a time for meditating here and there, or you often have to meditate in a different place, then rituals can help add some consistency.

FINDING THE RIGHT PLACE

As I mentioned before, the ideal place for meditation is quiet, clutter-free and consistent. It's worth taking some time to think about which area of your house is most conducive to meditation. This may depend on who is at home when you meditate. I dream of building a dedicated space for meditation in the garden: in the meantime I have to make do with our bedroom. Be prepared to change your space if the need arises. When we are between lodgers, I like to meditate in our spare attic bedroom, as it's tidy and quiet. When my son was a toddler, he found it very difficult to learn not to interrupt my meditation. In desperation I appealed to my community and one of my neighbours offered to lend me her empty house on weekday mornings.

TUNING OUT THE CHILDREN

I've always found one of the hardest aspects of meditating while children are in the house is that I get drawn into their noise. Parents have evolved to be on high alert to sounds from their children, especially distress signals, so it's no surprise that these sounds are incredibly distracting. Don't beat yourself up if you are finding it difficult to stay on task. My practical suggestions are: try to find a meditation spot that is out of earshot (preferably in another building!); failing that, use earplugs.

When the twins were tiny, I would leave them with their Dad and go and sit to practise for 30 minutes. I found it SO difficult to stay put, especially if I heard them cry but I knew it was important to let them feel safe with their dad (which they did) and it was my anxiety and possessiveness that made me want to run to them. I think I would have had massive arguments with my husband if I had not learnt to trust him with them.

Anne, mum to Stephen, 24, Clare, 24, Helen, 23, and Sarah, 20

Another thing to consider is whether you are actually trying to do two things at once (i.e. listen out for your children while you meditate). If that's the case, it may help to think about how you hand over responsibility to your partner, or whoever is looking after them when you sit. Perhaps it would help to agree beforehand situations when the other adult should interrupt you, for example if the baby is hungry, or a toddler is inconsolable. Once that has been decided you may find it easier to stop listening out, as you know that someone will tell you if there is an emergency.

If your baby is very young, or if you are the only adult in the house while your children watch TV or are asleep, then it may be necessary to keep half an ear out for them. If so, then accept that and work with it. It's hard to meditate in those conditions, but that doesn't mean it's not beneficial.

DEALING WITH INTERRUPTIONS

Sometimes the children will come and find you and disturb you while you sit. Or, it may be that other events such as the phone or the doorbell interrupt you. It's very tempting to abandon a sit once this has happened, but actually learning how to transition in and out of meditation is a very important skill. This is exactly the type of suppleness of mind that we are aiming to develop. My meditation teacher taught me that if I have to put down my practice halfway through, then I should try to do so in a way that means I can pick it up again once I have dealt with the interruption. It may help to pause momentarily before you come out of the meditation, and observe what's happening in the mind. Do you feel irritation? If so, notice it arise and fall away. Try to come out of the meditation with maximum awareness. If your meditation has stages, you may like to briefly go back a stage as a stepping-stone for exiting.

Usually he wakes up before I have finished and I have
to let the practice go.
Gareth, dad to Andrew, 6

BEING PRAGMATIC

It's very important to remember that establishing and maintaining a daily sitting practice is extremely challenging as a parent. Don't feel inadequate that you are 'not doing it properly'. It seems to me that there is an inverse correlation – the more challenging it is to keep it up – the more chaotic and noisy and stressful things are – the more beneficial it is to try to instil a little bit of calm in the day. By making a commitment to spend time attending to your own needs – which in turn helps those around you – you are doing an extraordinary thing.

Now and again it's worth checking that you really are setting up the very best conditions for your practice that you possibly can. Sometimes it's easy to stay stuck in old routines, when a fresh look, or even just a few tweaks, might bring a lot of benefit. However, be fair to yourself when it really isn't possible to make the environment more conducive. Then, you need to embrace things as they are, and do the best you can. If you can build up a practice in these kinds of conditions, then you will create a really solid one. And, when the time comes for you to be able to meditate in more conducive conditions – whether that's on retreat, or when the children are older – then you will be able to draw from all of that experience to pull out something very strong indeed. And, in the meantime, you'll reap the benefits of being more resourceful and calm.

I usually get up at 6 a.m. to make time to practise, but even then I don't always get that time alone and I've done a lot of formal practice with my youngest lying in my lap or breastfeeding.

Guin, MBCP meditation teacher and mum of three

SUMMARY

- *'Ideal conditions' meditation and 'adverse conditions' meditation may look very different, but you will be practising the same skills in both.*
- *It's best to practise at the same time and place every day, but if that's not possible then there's no need to worry. Using rituals can help to provide consistency.*

- *Give yourself permission to prioritise meditation. This is easier the more you appreciate how formal practice benefits you and the family as a whole.*
- *Be honest with yourself: can you make conditions more conducive? Even when it seems difficult there are often little things you can do to make it easier to practise.*
- *If you can't make the conditions more conducive, then just work with whatever space and time you do have.*

14

The Importance of Community

Developing mindfulness is a part of a quest for personal psychological growth. It offers us a system for increasing our self-awareness and openness and also considers how that can be applied to the benefit of the world around us. When you set out to practise mindfulness, you are essentially committing to making yourself 'a better person'. What that means exactly will be different to each of us – perhaps you want to enjoy life more, be more compassionate, less stressed, be more conscious, work more effectively, live more harmoniously with others – or all of these things and more.

In times gone by, the established religion would have offered both a system and a community in which to better ourselves. Nowadays in the West, our religious identities are much less fixed. Church-going is no longer a central part of most people's lives or they may feel disconnected to the religion in which they were raised. So, many of us find ourselves with a desire for self-exploration and improvement, but no framework to practise it in.

WHY DO WE NEED COMMUNITY?

It is absolutely clear that when we seek support from each other, we are more likely to achieve our goals. We can see this all over the place, when we go jogging with friends, join a Facebook group for knitting enthusiasts, sign up to Weight Watchers – the list is endless. Like-minded friends can offer us support and encouragement. They can make the journey more enjoyable.

Practising mindfulness is no different. Everyone who wants to pursue meditation can benefit from a community of like-minded friends, but I think parents are in *especial* need of support and encouragement.

ATTENDING A CLASS: TYPES OF CLASSES

As I already mentioned in Chapter 12 (see page 187), there are many different types of formal meditation practice. And this is reflected in the different types of classes on offer. Besides the differences in the actual meditation, classes and groups also fall into different categories to meet differing needs.

I would say that there are three main types of organizations offering meditation classes:

1. RELIGIOUS OR SPIRITUAL GROUPS

Until the last decade or so, the only way to access meditation teaching was through the outreach activities of religious and spiritual communities. Buddhist temples led by monks who have come to live or stay in the West are normally associated with a temple or monastery in the East (Thailand, Tibet or Sri Lanka, for example). They often have a following from Thai or Sri Lankan residents (for instance) in the community, though Westerners are welcome too. The temples often run meditation and chanting evenings that are open to the public.

There are also a number of meditation groups in the Buddhist tradition that have been formed in the West, and these may feel more accessible to Westerners. The Triratna Buddhist Order is one of the best known of these (you can find a list of such organizations in the appendix, see page 244). These groups tend to run regular classes for beginners and also sitting groups for more experienced meditators. Classes may be organized into courses of a certain length, or they may be drop-in. They normally also run residential retreats, either at their own centres or in hired venues.

Buddhism is not a belief-based religion – i.e. Buddhists are not required to believe or accept anything that contradicts their experience or reasoning – so joining a Buddhist group does not have to conflict with your established religious stance. Buddhism is not a missionary religion, in that it doesn't seek new converts, and you will be welcome to attend meditation classes whether you see yourself as a Buddhist or not.

The teaching offered by these groups may be of extremely high quality, with teachers who have an extensive personal practice and perhaps many decades of teaching experience. Such groups normally place great emphasis on lineage, with each teacher having his or her own teacher or guru.

In the main, both temples and meditation groups are run as charities, and their classes are often free or by donation. Generosity is normally seen as an important aspect of practice in these groups, and in time meditators will often demonstrate their commitment and gratitude by contributing in some way to the running of these groups or temples.

2. HEALTH AUTHORITIES AND INSTITUTIONS

In the last 10 years, more and more health-care providers have started offering secular mindfulness, as part of their mental health and wellbeing programmes. The MBSR programme developed by Jon Kabat-Zinn at the University of Massachusetts Medical School is now offered in over 200 medical centres, hospitals and clinics around the world. In the UK, similar courses are funded or part-funded by the NHS, and are available to specific groups of people, such as pregnant women (see page 211) or those suffering from depression. Normally, however, there is a charge.

These courses are proving extremely popular. Although the cost of each class is high, it is comparative to say, the cost of a psychotherapy session, or perhaps a massage. The fact that these courses are completely secular and stripped of any type of cultural associations is part of their appeal. The somewhat anonymous nature of them makes them feel accessible. Although meditators are certainly expected to make a personal commitment to their practice, they are not expected to set out the chairs, for example, or bring offerings of biscuits or flowers, and there won't be any hint of bowing or chanting. The courses tend to run for a set number of weeks, with participants expected to attend all the sessions. Often there is no framework for further teaching after the end of the course. Meditators who join these classes are essentially paying for a service, and so they may not develop the same degree of commitment to the class, and therefore the practice, in the way that the spiritual groups help to cultivate a sense of community.

In the main, teachers who have been trained to deliver secular mindfulness teach these types of classes. It's worth checking on the credentials of the teachers themselves, though hopefully the organization offering the course will have done this for you. These same teachers may offer classes privately (see below).

I should mention here that there are also groups that somewhat straddle the gap between these types of classes. At Oxford University in the UK, for example, students have formed a drop-in sitting group for meditators, taught by qualified secular mindfulness teachers. It's open to the public, and charges a small fee per session to cover costs. Its aim is to provide on-going community support. I imagine that this type of group is unlikely to exist outside of universities, and possibly some larger workplaces.

3. PRIVATE TEACHERS

In recent years there has also been an increase in the number of private teachers offering mindfulness classes, either as one-to-one or group classes, or perhaps as training days in the workplace. I define this group of teachers as those who consider teaching to be their 'work', and who charge accordingly. (In contrast to meditation teachers who are part of a wider community or school, who may offer their teaching for free or by donation.) There is a great range in the skills and experience of these teachers. Teachers may have many years of personal practice and teaching experience; they may have studied and practised under teachers from the East; or they may have completed a rigorous and lengthy training course (such as that offered by the Oxford Mindfulness Centre, UK, or the Center for Mindfulness at the University of Massachusetts Medical School). It is equally possible that they have attended a single day's training session. It's pretty impossible to give an overview of what these classes might be like, as there is a huge range.

MINDFULNESS FOR CHILDBIRTH

The pioneering Californian midwife Nancy Bardacke has developed a mindfulness programme specifically for expectant parents to help them with the challenges of pregnancy, childbirth and parenting. She adapted Jon Kabat-Zinn's well-known MBSR course to create the nine-week Mindfulness–based Childbirth and Parenting (MBCP) programme. Bardacke says that, 'teaching mindfulness during pregnancy creates the potential for promoting a healthy pregnancy and childbirth, and lays the foundation for lifelong skills for mindfully parenting the next generation.' Bardacke has worked with the Oxford Mindfulness Centre to bring MBCP to the UK, and trains MBCP instructors worldwide.

It is exciting that such a robust programme has been developed with the specific needs of expectant parents in mind, and that in the UK it is being brought into the mainstream through the NHS. It is expected that the opportunity to take this course will become more widely available as more MBCP teachers become trained. Hopefully it heralds the beginning of further work in developing mindfulness classes for parents.

An expectant father in one class admitted at the beginning to being skeptical about this new approach and apprehensive about what might be involved. However, he saw the course through, and at the end he told us that he came to the course for his partner, and then experimented with the practice for his unborn baby and was now practising before work for himself too to help with the stress of his job. I find stories like this inspiring, because it shows how transformational the course can be for people. They come looking for some support with the birth, but they leave with a skill that's applicable in many areas of their lives. It also shows how everyday and down to earth the practice of mindfulness can be. It's such a huge opportunity for people and a real privilege to play a part in offering this.

Maret Dymond, teacher/trainer of the MBCP programme
at the Oxford Mindfulness Centre

BUDDHIST MINDFULNESS VS. SECULAR MINDFULNESS

In the Buddhist world, there is some reservation about whether secular mindfulness teachers can impart the full significance of mindfulness, once stripped of its spiritual context. Likewise, some secular mindfulness teachers are suspicious of the lack of transparency in the teaching and training of teachers in a religious organization. Secular mindfulness teachers and training institutions place emphasis on the scientific, evidence-based approach. In contrast, spiritual meditation centres tend to emphasize the importance of *lineage* – the handing down of knowledge from teacher to teacher. Spiritual teachers tend to view mindfulness as a vehicle that must be harnessed in the path toward enlightenment, whereas secular teachers may consider the acquisition of mindfulness to be an end point in itself.

I think that the rise in popularity of both spiritual and secular mindfulness in recent years indicates that there is a need for *both* types of classes. When we set out to find a mindfulness class, we come from a certain cultural and social context. Some people are only able to consider accessing a class that has nothing to do with religion or spirituality. For others, this would render the teaching empty and invalid. The interesting thing about mindfulness is that it encourages us to be open-minded, to see things as they really are, without preconceptions. So whichever type of class appeals to you at the beginning, you may find that your needs change as you develop your practice.

However, it's probably true to say that the vast majority of new meditators choose their class primarily on convenience: whether it's in the right location, on the right day, or because their friend recommended it.

CHECKING CREDENTIALS

I don't want to sound overly cautious. I think it's absolutely fine to attend a taster session in mindfulness offered by an unknown teacher at a festival, for example.

However, if you are intending to make a significant commitment to a class or teacher (whether that's financial, a time commitment or in terms of your emotional investment), then I think it is important to understand exactly what the teacher's experience and/or qualifications are. Teachers should be transparent about how long they have been practising, who they learnt meditation from, and whether they are supported in the form of on-going mentoring, teaching or supervision.

If you are accessing a class run by a spiritual group, at some point it will be important to do a little research into the philosophy of the wider organization. When was the community formed, and by who? Does it consider itself part of a wider religious tradition? How is the community organized? Is the written teaching freely available? Does the community have links with other communities (perhaps monks or temples, for example)? Does the organization espouse any views that make you feel uncomfortable? In short – please check that you aren't about to join a cult!

THE BENEFITS OF A CLASS

But please don't think that meditation classes are likely to be dangerous brainwashing places that will ask you to rewrite your will or run by charlatans who are parroting what they read in a magazine last week. I think that a good class is an *invaluable* resource in establishing and maintaining a mindfulness practice. I would go so far as to say it is extremely difficult to keep up a practice without the support of a class or community. A class can offer many benefits – these are the four main ones:

- a teacher
- like-minded friends
- motivation
- commitment

A TEACHER

A teacher can take you through the technicalities of the meditation practice offered and can guide your individual practice as you develop. The way that they speak and act may also provide you with a model for mindful living. If he or she is part of a lineage or school, then that provides a context for your meditation and connects you to a wider community of meditators, beyond your own class.

LIKE-MINDED FRIENDS

It is very supportive just to be among friends who share your purpose. Hanging out with other people who do the same thing makes us feel normal. And when you actually discuss practice, you can learn so much from each other, sharing wisdom and experience.

MOTIVATION

Knowing that you will be attending a regular class can help to keep you motivated to try to keep up your practice in between times. At class, you may refer to your personal meditation and draw from your experience. In some schools, your teacher may have individual meetings with you to help you develop your practice. Again, this provides additional motivation to keep it up, as you may not want to admit you haven't done your 'homework'!

*The classes were a huge help with learning and building
up momentum in meditation practice.*
Ed, dad to Ruth, 9

COMMITMENT

When you attend a class you are making an outward sign of your commitment to your practice. You are acknowledging to others, but more significantly to yourself, that your meditation practice is important enough to warrant heading out each week or each fortnight (or whatever), to help sustain it. This works as a positive feedback cycle. The more you attend, the more committed you become.

Also, you are gaining from the commitment of others – your fellow meditators have also made the effort to come, and the teacher who is leading the class has committed to being there, perhaps giving their time for free. This encourages us to make a reciprocal commitment to both the class and our personal practice.

*It's wonderful when I go. What I like most is the sharing
circle at the end. It's amazing to hear how other people's
discoveries or difficulties reflect and inform your own.*
Ben, dad to Leo, 6

THE PRACTICALITIES OF ATTENDING A CLASS

So we've established that there are multiple benefits to be had from attending a class. But how exactly do you go about doing that? For one thing – there may not be a class in your area. The other problem that most parents face is the difficulty of going out in the evening. I think this can be especially hard for mothers with babies under a year. Although it's not the case in all families, mothers often find themselves in great demand in the evening.

I had been attending a class for a couple of years before I had my son, so I was keen to start going again as soon as I could. Because I was breastfeeding him, I felt that it was unrealistic to try to go out in the evening without him during the first six months. I also had the added problem that I needed to switch to a new class within the same school, as my old class had stopped running. When he was seven months old, and didn't need feeding so often, I decided to try again. I told my new teacher that I would start attending again. I gave my son a good feed, and either left him asleep, or awake with Dad, who also had to put our three-year-old daughter to bed.

It soon became apparent my family was paying too high a price for my attendance. I would often leave the house with both children wailing and poor Dad looking stressed. Sometimes I would return after 10 p.m. to find my son still awake and crying. Although I had hoped that my going out might lead to both my husband and son gaining more confidence in doing bedtime without me, the reality was that it wasn't working out. I threw in the towel and told my new teacher not to expect me for another few months.

It was a frustrating time for me and I felt very isolated in my meditation practice. I found it very hard to sustain a daily formal sit without the support of a teacher and class. It wasn't until my son was about 18 months old that I found it possible to make a regular commitment to class.

If going out in the evening is too difficult, this doesn't necessarily mean you need to forgo attending a class. There are other possibilities that may help provide a community.

LOOK FOR DAY CLASSES

It may be that you can find a class that operates at a better time for your family. Some centres organize classes that run in the daytime – particularly at the weekend. Perhaps you can ask your partner, family member or a friend to look after your child while you attend.

VISIT A TEMPLE

Most Buddhist temples are very welcoming of children. A monk once told me that in Sri Lanka, the main reason people visit temples is to bring their children – as they want to educate them. Temples in the West may even have special days when children are particularly welcome, or you may be able to simply drop in and meditate with your children in tow.

FAMILY GROUPS WITH A SIMILAR SLANT

In towns and cities it is often possible to find groups aimed at mother and baby, such as family yoga or baby massage. While these may not be exactly what you are looking for, they may have an element of meditation involved in the activity. More importantly, they could help you to meet like-minded people – which leads on to the next idea:

TIP: Start your own group!

Why not gather together two or three friends who also want to meditate and start meeting regularly at a time that suits you. You could bring your babies along, or meet at a time when you can leave them more easily.

TELL YOUR TEACHER OR SCHOOL WHAT IT IS YOU NEED

If you are already used to going to a particular group or class, but now find it difficult to attend because of your new addition, then it may be worth explaining your position. If your teacher understands your situation, he or she may be able to come up with some suggestions – perhaps allowing you to maintain contact with them by email or phone, by suggesting a class which you *could* attend, or perhaps even by adapting a group so that babies can attend too.

FIND A MEDITATION GROUP FOR PARENTS

I've got to be honest, there are not many of these around. I have helped to set up a mindful parenting group in my local town, with a mindfulness teacher who trained with the Oxford Mindfulness Centre. In our group we have a formal sit, followed by discussion of an aspect of parenting, and how that relates to mindfulness. Children are welcome, and we accept that there will be a certain amount of disturbance due to their presence. We have found that *allowing* the children to be as they are during the session is actually a fundamental part of this practice. Of course, the group can't meet everyone's complete needs, but it goes some way toward meeting some of them. Such groups are few and far between, but hopefully, in time, they will become more available.

The group is also a gentle reminder to be as mindful as I can for the rest of week. Life is so busy as a parent that I need regular reminders to come back to myself; unfortunately a meditation practice would be low down on the list of priorities if it weren't for the group, despite theoretically knowing that the benefits would help in a myriad of ways not just for myself but for Alba too.

Gemma, mum to Alba, 8 months

FIND AN ONLINE COMMUNITY

Nowadays there is a huge amount of material available online, including actual courses, with real teachers and virtual classrooms. As with choosing a real-life class, make sure that the course or organization is a reputable one. Don't be too convinced by the web design: slick websites don't always go hand in hand with a wealth of experience and skill.

You may also find community in peer-to-peer forums such as Facebook groups and blogs. It's possible to find groups that are specifically dedicated to mindful parenting on these platforms.

SUMMARY

- *You are much more likely to succeed in establishing and maintaining a mindfulness practice if you do it as part of a community.*

- *Mindfulness classes fall into two main categories: those teaching secular mindfulness and those teaching Buddhist mindfulness. Although they present mindfulness in different contexts, the meditation teaching itself may be very similar.*

- *Always check you are comfortable with the credentials and philosophy of any class that you attend.*

- *A class can offer you support from a teacher, the community of fellow meditators, increased motivation and commitment.*

- *It can be difficult to attend an evening class when you have young children who need you at bedtime. Find creative solutions for accessing teaching and community.*

15

Going on Retreat

Just as a formal daily sit can both strengthen and deepen your practice, so too can a period of retreat. However, if you find it hard to make space for a daily sit, you may find it even harder to allow for a retreat that lasts several days. However, retreats can play an important and pivotal role in developing your practice, so it's useful to consider how (and when) we can incorporate them into family life.

WHAT IS A RETREAT?

The word retreat is used in many different contexts – such as yoga retreat, writers' retreat, spa retreat, and we may have preconceptions about what goes on. A meditation retreat is a fixed period of time when meditators join together, normally at a residential centre, to focus on their meditation practice. The programme is led by a teacher or teachers, and may include theoretical talks, periods of mindful work, walking, and, of course, lots of group and individual practice. The retreat may be themed, to explore a specific aspect of practice or teaching.

The clue is in the name. During a retreat, you will literally be removed from your everyday life. Work, family, friends, social engagements, hobbies, classes, activities, responsibilities and roles: all of these will be put on hold for the duration of the retreat. Of course, you will assume new responsibilities and roles while you are away – you may be asked to do mindful work (perhaps cooking or gardening), you will certainly be required to dedicate yourself to practice, and you will be asked to make sure that your behaviour, including your speech (or more likely silence), is conducive to the work of your fellow meditators.

BENEFITS OF RETREATS

I think retreats benefit us in two distinct ways: one is that they offer us the opportunity to do lots of practice; the other is that they provide the opportunity to refrain from doing everything else. For example, you will probably be asked to forgo reading while you are on retreat. If you are anything like me, you will obediently pack your books away ... but then find yourself reading every little scrap of writing in sight: from yoghurt pots and cereal boxes, to the fire escape notice and the microwave settings. The great thing about retreats is that we start to notice these funny habits of mind – the things that we do when there isn't anything to do. Once we have noticed them, we can ask ourselves: why? This kind of close examining can teach us an awful lot about ourselves.

And then there's the practice itself. When we *really* commit to spending a few hours a day to being mindful, and have the opportunity to do so without any distractions, then we can forge some really powerful habits of the mind. Turning our attention back to the breath, again and again and again, is a bit like exercising a muscle. The brain gets so used to this action, that turning our attention back to the breath becomes effortless – a way of being, even. We get so used to being mindful that it becomes our default state – one that we can bring back with us when we return to our everyday lives – at least for a bit, anyway!

I went to Plum Village [*a retreat centre*] a few years ago. I found it a challenging and life-changing experience, as I learned to be mindful and deal with difficult emotions in a place without distractions.
Kate, mum to Zach, 2½

WHO OFFERS RETREATS?

At the moment, most retreats are run by long-established meditation centres, normally as part of a spiritual tradition. Also, many Buddhist monasteries offer public retreats as part of their annual schedule. As secular mindfulness is still in its infancy these retreats are harder to find, but secular organizations may have links with existing spiritual retreat centres, which offer compatible meditation programmes. The Oxford Mindfulness Centre, for example, has a history of collaboration with Gaia House in Devon, a Buddhist retreat centre. Likewise, teachers training at The Centre for Mindfulness often attend retreats at the Insight Meditation Society, MA, USA. (You can find a list of retreat centres on page 244.)

If you are thinking of going on a retreat, it is really important to choose one led by an experienced and competent teacher. The work involved in leading a retreat is highly skilled. You should feel absolutely confident in your retreat leader. In an ideal world, your retreat centre will be part of the same group that you meditate with, or at least the same type of meditation. If your meditation class is not attached to a wider organization with its own centre, perhaps your class teacher can recommend a centre, or perhaps a specific retreat that will be suitable for you. Most retreat leaders will be quite precise about who their retreat is aimed at; some may specify a number of years of practice, for example, or that you have been on a certain number of previous retreats. I do think that it is helpful to consult with your own teacher, if possible.

WHEN TO GO ON RETREAT

When time is precious, going on retreat may not be at the top of your list of things to do. If you are considering leaving the kids with grandma for the weekend, you might be more inclined to go away for a romantic break with your partner, go for a spa weekend with friends, or go to a festival perhaps. I think that the desire to work more deeply with your practice is something that grows over time. As practice gets more firmly established, and we become more aware of the benefits, then gradually our priorities might shift until going on retreat takes on a broader significance. It matters to us more.

Having said that, I have known people who, without any established meditation practice, suddenly decide to go on a week-long silent retreat. I find this slightly alarming! To me, building up a practice takes time, dedication and patience. The drip, drip, drip approach helps establish something really solid and long lasting. Signing up for an intense week's retreat as a complete beginner suggests something of a boot-camp mentality: *find yourself in just seven days!* Having said that, some people who have followed this route have undoubtedly found that jumping in at the deep end is the best motivation to pick up a practice. They needed that blast right at the beginning, to give them enough momentum to carry on.

I personally prefer a more cautious approach, which is to build up a daily practice alongside the attendance of a class. When you feel committed to the practice, perhaps after a year or so, then that may be a good time to consider going on a retreat. Of course, it may just be that I had no choice about the matter: I took up meditation when my daughter was 18 months old, and I didn't feel that I was in a position to be able to leave her overnight for almost another 18 months – let alone go away for a full week. Who knows what I would have done had I been free and single.

When I discussed this with my teacher (in the context of going on a week-long retreat), he explained that a week's retreat does the job of consolidating an existing practice. There is an optimum window – too early, and a meditator would not have acquired enough material to gather from, yet too late and they would be holding back their practice. This ideal window may extend over a relatively long time – perhaps one to six years into the practice, depending on the meditator.

BUT HOW CAN I LEAVE MY CHILDREN?

Deciding whether and when to leave your children can be extremely daunting – especially because when we leave them to go on retreat, we are not merely a phone call and a short drive away if something goes wrong. (Or, even if we are, we have made a commitment to cut off communication for the duration.) I think it is fair to say that this decision tends to be harder for mothers, and it is especially difficult for breastfeeding mothers. Therefore the following discussion is aimed more at mothers (and fathers if they are the primary carer).

Being closely and firmly attached to your child is an essential aspect in the raising of secure, confident children, who will grow into happy, healthy adults. 'Being there' for them is a fundamental part of the attachment process, and by this I mean both 'being there' as a physical presence through much of the day, day after day, and also 'being there' in a subtler way – being present and conscious with your children when they smile at you with delight, or suffer from discomfort or frustration. Going on retreat presents a paradoxical situation: it temporarily prevents us from 'being there' in a physical way for a few days, but it will greatly increase our capacity to 'be there' in a mindful way, once we have returned.

So we need to strike a balance between these two factors. In the main, the importance of 'being there' consistently as a physical presence, will diminish as your child grows. However, it's important not to underestimate how important you are.

PREPARING FOR MY FIRST RETREAT

After I had completed my first year of practice, my teacher recommended that I should go on retreat for a weekend or few days. Although I was keen to try it, I felt that it would be *impossible* to leave my daughter. She was two-and-a-half, and I had never left her overnight before. My reluctance to leave her was undoubtedly compounded by the fact that I still breastfed her at bedtime and in the morning. Although I no longer gave her milk during the night, she still woke up, and relied upon my presence to go back to sleep. Despite the fact that she had a very close relationship with her father, only I would do in the night. The thought of leaving her crying in the night was terrible to me, and I was sure that I would not be able to relax and embrace the retreat with this worry. I agonized over the decision for weeks. I discussed with teachers the possibility of me installing my husband and daughter in the vicinity, and me returning to them at nighttime. But in the end I felt that I would be better to wait until we were ready.

By the time my daughter was two years and eight months, I felt that I could risk leaving her. I did a trial run a couple of weeks in advance and spent a night away. Dad and daughter coped fine, so I was all set to go for my weekend retreat.

LEAVING THE CHILDREN: FINDING THE RIGHT TIME

Many years ago, I was discussing the difficulties of going to the hairdresser when parenting a young baby. A friend described the relationship she had with her baby by referring to Philip Pullman's book *Northern Lights*.[30] In his fantasy novel, people are basically the same as us humans, except that a part of their personality or soul resides in an animal that always accompanies them. These animals, known as 'dæmons', are attached to their person by an invisible bond, and they are unable to travel more than a few metres away from them. Tearing the dæmon and person apart causes indescribable pain and suffering, and leaves the damaged person a helpless shell.

This comparison of the mother and baby with Pullman's people and their dæmons really resonated with me. When I was separated from my small baby, even just for a couple of hours, I felt the separation as an actual ache in my chest. And, in contrast, when I was in the company of my baby (i.e. pretty much the rest of the time) it was as if there was a warm glowing light that transmitted between us – that is, if I took the time to be mindful and notice it. I distinctly remember once cycling along with my then nine-month-old son strapped into the bike seat on the back, and noticing that his simple presence there made me feel happy and complete.

I am a firm believer that the attachment that exists between parent and child makes its presence felt in both directions. Most new mothers would find it very difficult to be separated from their newborn for a prolonged period. This desire to stay close by protects the baby in its vulnerable state. I am sure that this attunement between parent and baby (and especially mother and baby), where the baby's unarticulated fears are reflected in the parent's emotions, is nature's mechanism for ensuring a baby's wellbeing. I think that fathers have the equal capacity to feel this attunement. However, they may find it easier to be away from baby, because their fears are allayed by the knowledge that their baby is in the safe hands of the mother. In cases where mothers are unable to look after their babies, then fathers may experience intense anxiety. This mechanism doesn't go away as babies gets older, but it exerts a weaker pull, and it may be harder to recognize it.

This internal barometer of our child's neediness means that parents themselves are the very best people to judge when their children are ready to be left. We also need to factor in how important the trip will be for our own welfare, and what consequences it might have for the family. For example, we might be prepared to leave a 12-month-old overnight to go into hospital, but would forgo a hen weekend. Of course it will be difficult to know exactly how a retreat might benefit you, especially the first one.

After a week of strict practice I remember coming home and having Helen on my knee in the garden in the sunshine and just enjoying her completely, nothing else mattered: her chuckling, her joy at playing with me, our connectedness, our love, feeling carefree.

Anne, mum to Stephen, 24, Clare, 24, Helen, 23,
and Sarah, 20

Although breastfeeding is often cited as an obstacle to leaving your child, I think we need to examine this idea a little more thoroughly, and consider why that might be the case. Health authorities promoting breastfeeding are quick to point out that a mother can express milk to allow her to be away from her baby. Although not quite so optimum, a baby's diet can also be supplemented with formula feeds. Older babies may source much of their diet from solid foods. In short, it is possible to meet a baby's nutritional needs for a couple of days without the mother being present.

However, in reality, many breastfeeding mothers find that their absence is distressing for their baby, who may reject a bottle. It's unrealistic to suppose that a bottle can be a substitute for a mother's reassuring presence. The breastfeeding relationship brings the mother-baby bond into sharper focus and helps to protect it, but bottle-fed babies can also find their mother's absence distressing. All babies, whether bottle- or breast-fed have a need for a consistent attachment figure.

When I went on my first retreat (for two nights) I was still breastfeeding my daughter. Although I was concerned about whether she would miss the feeds, I felt that the bigger question was whether she would miss me. I wanted to be as sure as I could that while she might be sad, she wouldn't be distraught. I knew that her Dad could help her process any difficulty. I hoped we had given her a sound enough foundation that any pain she now felt could be absorbed and used for growth, rather than cause damage and limitation. So although breastfeeding was a factor in my decision, it wasn't a reason in itself not to go.

Instead of using a tick list (what age is she, is she breastfeeding etc.), I had to carefully imagine what the experience of the weekend would be like for her and look deeply inside myself to see if she would be able to manage that. If she had been 10 weeks old, I could have said no instantly. At seven years old, I also barely give it a moment's thought. She might prefer me to stay around, but she certainly has the resources to manage without me. As attached parents, we ourselves know when the time is right or at least – we tend to have a pretty good sense about it. And there is bound to be a fair amount of leeway, as children are flexible beings.

We also have to factor in the length of the retreat. While I felt comfortable leaving my almost three-year-old son for two nights, I was much more cautious about leaving him for longer. I recognized that I was very keen to go for a week to develop my practice, and I was unclear whether this desire was clouding my judgement. I even signed up for a week and then pulled out, when the reality of leaving him for so long hit home. When I eventually did go, my son was aged four, and long since weaned. I had few qualms about the separation, and felt that the net benefit to the family would be worth it. When I returned home, my husband reported that the week had passed without mishap or drama, and both children had seemed to cope fine. However, my son was unusually angry and aggressive over the next few days.

I asked him how he had felt when I was away, and he explained: 'Each day was 130 hours to get to bedtime, and you still didn't come.' Because he was able to articulate, I had a sudden insight into his experience: having to endure the waiting, day after day, with each day seeming to take forever to pass, not really understanding when I would finally arrive, half wondering if it might be that afternoon, or the next day, and being continually disappointed. Of course, the concept of a week itself was beyond him; he would not have been able to calculate how far through he was. We cuddled and allowed that ache to resonate between us. I hope he felt heard, and that it went some way toward releasing his pain.

Would I have done it a second time round? It was hard for him to bear my absence, and I acknowledged that to both of us. I accepted that he was more clingy and sensitive over the following week, and he soon regained his buoyant self, perhaps even more confident than before. The benefits to me, and indeed the family as a whole, were immense. So yes, I would do it again. I intend to go again in a year's time, and my son will have a better idea about how long a week feels. He'll also be a year older.

SEIZING OPPORTUNITIES TO EMBRACE CHANGE

As parents, we tend to form habits around our day-to-day routines. These are instrumental in helping our children feel confident and grounded. For example: at bedtime, one parent or another might supervise bath time, read a story, lie with the child or tuck her up. These predictable patterns are soothing for all of us, allowing us to reserve our mental energy for other less predictable goings-on. However, routines can become so ingrained, that we don't notice our children have outgrown the need for us to act in a certain way. We may be inadvertently holding them back. It's good to check in occasionally to see if we need to change our routines to keep pace with our children's development.

I have often found that chance events provide a catalyst for change. For example, the washing machine breaking down might spark toilet training. Your teacher recommending a retreat might offer an opportunity to spend a longer period away from the children. I even found that going on a three-night retreat presented an opportunity for me to peacefully wean my son. Trying to say no to breastfeeding while I was still at home would have been much more painful for the both of us, even though I was sure he was ready.

When they were younger I felt a week each year was not unreasonable and did this from when the youngest was 3. They stayed with grandparents and did not seem to miss me.

Deborah, meditation teacher and mum to Jesse, 20, and Rowan, 17

I'm not saying that you should let yourself be swept up in the course of events, without making considered decisions about your parenting. It's important that we don't give that impression to our children either: they need to know that we are in control. But sometimes chance events make us reflect on how things are going, and can nudge us into action. If some event has got you seriously considering toilet training, or weaning, or changing the bedtime routine, then perhaps it is the right time after all.

MAKING A MINDFUL CHOICE

The crucial point in deciding whether and when to go on a retreat, is that you need to be mindful about the differing needs of yourself, your child and the family as a whole. It is important to really try to imagine what the experience will be like for your child, so that you can gauge whether he is ready to manage it. Of course, you will never know for sure. To a certain extent, your leaving *will* be a compromise. It's perfectly possible that your being away will cause your child pain. Recognizing and allowing for that is an important part of both making a choice and to promote healing when you return.

You may feel that your child is ready for you to leave him for a few days at two years old, or it may be three years, or four. Only *you* know your child best.

WHEN YOU CAN'T LEAVE YOUR CHILD

Although there's nothing quite like a residential fixed length retreat, with a bit of creativity, you may be able to find other ways to deepen your practice. When I've discussed this with other meditators, they sometimes have the view that I simply need to be patient – it's only for a couple of years. This doesn't satisfy me, however! With the experience of two children, I have found so far that my internal barometer allows me to go away for a weekend at around the three-year mark, and for a week at around four years. Given that my tradition really emphasizes the importance of weeklong retreats, that's a lot of time spent being patient.

I've therefore found it really valuable to find other ways to concentrate on my practice, without compromising the needs of my children.

DAY RETREATS

Retreats that run over the course of a single day are a lovely way to focus on practice while remaining available at bedtime. Although some meditators find these quite challenging, as it may be difficult to 'let yourself go' in such a short space of time, I have normally found them to be very helpful. You may have the opportunity to learn different types of practice – perhaps walking and standing meditation, and to spend a longer period of time with other meditators. You may do perhaps four or five formal sits, which will help to consolidate your everyday practice.

TIP: Turning up the volume on your individual practice

If it is not possible to access any non-residential or day retreats, then another possibility is to simply dedicate some time to more intense practice by yourself. This could be in the form of meditating more frequently for a period – perhaps upping your meditation routine from one to two sits per day, for example. Or it could be setting aside a day or half-day for lots of sits in a row. If this idea appeals to you, then I think it is important to work out a plan in discussion with your teacher so that you are properly supported. It may be that fellow meditators would like to join you, which could provide a lovely opportunity for connecting with others.

NON-RESIDENTIAL RETREATS

Some centres offer non-residential retreats. For example, the Buddhist temple in my town runs four or five day retreats every month. Although they have some accommodation, local people normally return home each night. This can provide an excellent opportunity for a more intense period of practice. Of course, it is not exactly the same as breaking all contact with your everyday life, but it is a lot better than not doing anything at all.

FAMILY RETREATS

When my son was small, my practice was likewise still in its infancy, and I felt frustrated that I could not go on retreat. By chance my retreat centre in Wales organized a social event when my children were four and one. Families were invited to attend, and so we went along and camped for a couple of nights. While I was there I shared my difficulties about going on retreat with other parents of young children. I must have inspired some people because within a few months, the community I meditate with decided to pilot a family retreat.

Experienced meditators from within our group were invited to come for a three-day retreat, with partners and children in tow. I was asked to help organize it and have done ever since. The retreat offers space for both experienced and beginning meditators to practise together, and in time we have developed low-key activities for the children to join in with as well. Some of which relate to meditation and Buddhism, some are simply wholesome craft or outdoor activities. The families get to know each other at the same time as having an opportunity to practise together – free from (some of) the distractions of home.

It was here that my husband also began meditating and has since taken up his own practice. My children have now stayed at the retreat centre four times, and have come to hold it very dearly in their hearts. I have also found that it is much easier for my children to let me go on retreat by myself, as they can clearly imagine where I will be staying and what I might be doing. Though sometimes they complain that they are not allowed to come too!

It's hard to take part in the retreat to the same extent as other adults who are there without kids, and at times that has caused stress, as my wife and I have wanted to be more involved in all the retreat activities, but in the last two years I think we've finally managed to let go of that, and just do what we can. Then it's much easier, and we find that the most valuable thing of all is being with other parents and families on the same path. Being with and chatting to them is the most rewarding thing of all.

Ben, dad to Leo, 6

SUMMARY

- *Retreats provide an excellent opportunity to develop your practice. They provide time and space to meditate and remove ordinary distractions.*
- *Most retreats are run by long-established meditation centres. Ideally you can find one in the same tradition you normally meditate in.*
- *It can be very difficult to go on retreat when you have young children – especially for mothers.*
- *We need to consider our children's needs very carefully when deciding when to go. As firmly attached parents, we can sense when they might be able to do without us.*
- *If you can't leave your children overnight, you can practise more intensely at day retreats and non-residential retreats. Some retreat centres offer family retreats.*

Final Thoughts

Last year, when I was bemoaning the difficulty in partaking of a week's retreat, someone mentioned they had heard that in Buddhist countries, mothers don't go on retreat. Given that meditation has been handed to us from the East, it can be helpful to examine how aspects of meditation practice are traditionally managed in Buddhist countries, and why.

In fact, I was surprised to discover that in Buddhist countries such as Thailand and Sri Lanka, most lay people (of either sex) don't meditate regularly, let alone go on retreat. Instead, much of their practice is in the form of charity toward the monastics; visiting the temple and showing respect is an important part of their religious participation. Meditation itself is seen as the province of monks.

So what about nuns? I was amazed to find out that there aren't any! Well that's not quite true. However, there are certainly very few. The Buddha originally set up communities of both monks and nuns, but in the Southern Theravada tradition, the nuns had died out by the 13th century. Because the Buddha said that nuns have to be ordained by nuns, it meant that the tradition couldn't be revived. Many key Buddhist leaders such as HH Dalai Lama XIV have called for a restoration of the female *Sangha*, but it has been met with extreme difficulty. In Thailand, for example, nuns have no legal status at all, and currently only number about 30. For a long time the only country in the world offering full ordination for women was China.[31]

I think we have to understand that while the core teaching itself is gender neutral, it is clear that having evolved in patriarchal societies over two-and-a-half millennia, the practice has tended to favour men, who seem to find it easier to renounce worldly concerns and familial ties.

So how does all this relate to mindful parenting? The fact that Buddhism has always been applied and practised within patriarchal societies means it is less concerned with the needs and activities of women. That is not to say that Buddhism doesn't recognize the value of parenthood (and motherhood in particular): the teachings often refer positively to the relationship between mother and child. However, motherhood tends to be represented as a fixed archetype rather than as a vehicle for growth – and this is hardly surprising when the men who developed the tradition had literally turned their backs on family life through their vows of celibacy. Buddhism therefore tends to under-emphasize the needs of parents who want to pursue a spiritual practice, and likewise it doesn't tend to consider the special opportunities parenting presents.

Buddhist practice tends to emphasize the importance of solitary retreat for developing practice – and it is absolutely clear that retreats do deepen practice in a certain way. However, what has been less acknowledged is the value that can also be gained from a quieter, less intense practice, but by no means less dedicated – that of the parent consistently being present with his or her children. And I say *his or her*, because nowadays, in the West at least, the art of parenting is available to *both mothers and fathers*.

Practising mindful parenting requires a dedication and persistence that reaps enormous benefits. It also provides a natural, yet unique opportunity for cultivating the qualities of boundless love – loving-kindness, compassion, sympathetic joy and equanimity. Although these two different approaches (solitary retreat vs. family life) influences a meditation practice in different ways, I think that both are equally valid ways to develop.

What I've discovered over the years is that my practice
is actually very resilient, it's like a flickering fire that is
always burning even during times when the flames have
died right down, and it can be reignited very quickly ...
Basically it comes down to a rock-hard intention to make
it happen. It definitely helps to see it as an act of kindness
toward myself rather than one more thing I have to do.

Guin, MBCP meditation teacher and mum of three

So although in the last chapter I talked at length about the
benefits of retreats and how you might go on one, I don't want
to underestimate the value of a dedicated mindfulness practice
that takes place in the heart of the family. Practising in intense
retreat conditions can certainly move your practice forward in
a special way – but so can being present for your children, day
after day, year after year. Not only is parenting intense, it also
requires us to make a sustained – even lifelong – commitment.
Although there are (thankfully) times when our children are less
needy, and which allow us a little breathing space, ultimately
parenting demands a level of dedication that is unlike any other.
When we meet that challenge by continually opening our hearts
to our children, we are cultivating a very deep and powerful
practice indeed.

Buddhism tends to change wherever it goes and take on a
flavour of the people who practise it. This is the way people
make the philosophy relevant and applicable. The secular
mindfulness movement currently surging through the West
is a manifestation of this change. We Westerners, who have
in many ways rejected religion and spirituality in favour of
science and consumerism, have nevertheless understood the
value of Buddhist meditation, and adapted it to fit into our
modern world. Some practitioners still view it as a spiritual
path toward enlightenment. Others need to access it through
the context of evidence-based scientific understanding. As long

as we approach the practice with an open questioning mind, I don't think it matters much where we start.

I think that the growth of Buddhism in societies where men and women are closer in equality also has an impact on the way meditation is taught and practised. Valuing women leads to valuing the traditional work of women – that of parenting. But parenting is not something that is exclusive to women; *both* parents can use parenting as a powerful opportunity for growth. We can start to see ever more clearly that meditation is not just something that must be practised behind closed doors, away from responsibilities and away from other people – it can and must be practised right here, amidst the chaos of our everyday lives.

And when we do commit to bringing mindfulness right into the thick of our families and our lives, then we have a real chance to be the best parents, and the best people, that we can.

Notes on the Text

1. Gethin, R. 'On Some Definitions of Mindfulness', *Contemporary Buddhism*, 12 (2011), 263–79; http://dx.doi.org/10.1080/14639947.2011.564843

2. Williams, M., Teasdale, J., Segal, Z. and Kabat-Zinn, J. *The Mindful Way Through Depression: Freeing Yourself from Chronic Unhappiness*, 1 Pap/Com edition (New York: Guilford Press, 2007)

3. Williams, M. and Penman, D., *Mindfulness: A Practical Guide to Finding Peace in a Frantic World* (London: Piatkus, 2011)

4. Kabat-Zinn, J. and Kabat-Zinn, M., *Everyday Blessings: Mindfulness for Parents* (Piatkus, 2014), 98

5. Kabat-Zinn, J. and Kabat-Zinn, M. *Everyday Blessings: Mindfulness for Parents* (Piatkus, 2014), 92

6. Thich Nhat Hanh, *Peace Is Every Step: The Path of Mindfulness in Everyday Life*, (London: Rider, 1991)

7. http://www.sharonsalzberg.com/wishing-well/, accessed 24 May 2016

8. Thich Nhat Hanh, 'Love Without Frontiers', 25 November 2004 (Mindfulness Bell #70, autumn, 2015)

9. Flom, R., Lee, K. and Muir, D. eds., *Gaze-Following: Its Development and Significance*, 1st edition (Mahwah, NJ: Psychology Press, 2006)

10. Cohen, L. *Playful Parenting*, Reprint edition (New York: Ballantine Books, 2012)

11. González, C. *My Child Won't Eat!: How to Enjoy Mealtimes without Worry*, 2, revised and updated edition (London: Pinter & Martin Ltd., 2012)

12. Rapley, G. and Murkett, T. *Baby-Led Weaning: Helping Your Baby to Love Good Food* (London: Vermilion, 2008)

13. Chandra, S. *Banish Clutter Forever: How the Toothbrush Principle Will Change Your Life* (London: Vermilion, 2010)

14. Payne, K. *Simplicity Parenting: Using the Extraordinary Power of Less to Raise Calmer, Happier, and More Secure Kids* (New York: Ballantine Books Inc., 2010)

15. *Ibid*, 32

16. Takeuchi, H. *et al.* 'The impact of television viewing on brain structures: Cross-sectional and longitudinal analyses', *Cerebral Cortex*, May, 2015; 25, 1188–97

17. Rideout, V., Hamel, E. and the Kaiser Family Foundation, 2006, www.kff.org/entmedia/upload/7500.pdf – See more at: http://families. naeyc. org/learning-and-development/music-math-more/how-true-are-our-assumptions-about-screen-time#sthash.lb25lOB8.dpuf

18. Porter, J. Olsen, A. Gurnsey, K. Dugan, B. Jedema, H. and Bradberry, C. 'Chronic Cocaine Self-Administration in Rhesus Monkeys: Impact on Associative Learning, Cognitive Control, and Working Memory', *The Journal of Neuroscience*, 31 (2011), 4926–34, http://dx.doi.org/10.1523/ JNEUROSCI.5426-10.2011

19. http://www.mirror.co.uk/news/technology-science/technology/over-three-quarters-british-mums-6455379, accessed 9 June 2016

20. Faber, A. and Mazlish, E. *How To Talk So Kids Will Listen and Listen So Kids Will Talk*, Third edition (London: Piccadilly Press, 2013)

21. http://www.youtube.com/watch?v=MUO-pWJ0riQ, accessed 18 February 2016

22. Jackson, D. *Letting Go as Children Grow: From Early Intimacy to Full Independence – a Parent's Guide*, New edition (London: Bloomsbury Publishing PLC, 2003)

23. *Global Ethics for our Future*, 11 August 2010, Hammersmith Apollo, London

24. Salzberg, S. *Loving-kindness: The Revolutionary Art of Happiness*, Revised edition (Boston: Shambhala Publications Inc., 2002)

25. Claxton, G. *What's the Point of School? Rediscovering the Heart of Education*, Reprint edition (Richmond: Oneworld Publications, 2008)

26. Gold, E. 'Mindfulness with Children' in *Mindfulness Breakthrough: The Revolutionary Approach to Dealing with Stress, Anxiety and Depression* ed. Silverton, S. (London: Watkins Publishing Ltd, 2012)

27. Davidson, R. and Lutz, A. 'Buddha's Brain: Neuroplasticity and Meditation', *IEEE Signal Processing Magazine*, 25 (2008), 174–176

28. Thich Nhat Hanh, *The Miracle of Mindfulness: A Manual on Meditation* (London: Rider, 1991)

29. Williams, Mark, Teasdale, J., Segal, Z., and Kabat-Zinn, J., *The Mindful Way Through Depression: Freeing Yourself from Chronic Unhappiness*, 1 Pap/Com edition (New York: Guilford Press, 2007) pp. 78-79.

30. Pullman, P. *Northern Lights: His Dark Materials 1*, 1 edition (Scholastic, 2011)

31. Kabilsingh, C. *Thai Women in Buddhism*, 1st edition (Berkeley, Calif: Parallax Press, 1993)

Further Reading

MEDITATION/MINDFULNESS BOOKS FOR FAMILIES

Bardacke, Nancy, *Mindful Birthing: Training the Mind, Body, and Heart for Childbirth and Beyond*, Original edition (New York: Bravo Ltd, 2012)

Thich Nhat Hanh, *A Handful of Quiet: Happiness in Four Pebbles*, Crds edition (Berkeley, CA: Parallax Press, 2012)

Thich Nhat Hanh, and Plum Village Community, *Planting Seeds: Practicing Mindfulness with Children*, Pap/Com Or edition (Berkeley, CA: Parallax Press, 2011)

Kabat-Zinn, Jon, and Myla, *Everyday Blessings: Mindfulness for Parents* (Piatkus, 2014)

Napthali, Sarah, *Buddhism for Mothers: A Calm Approach to Caring for Yourself and Your Children* (Crows Nest, N.S.W.; London: Allen & Unwin, 2011)

Snel, Eline, *Sitting Still Like a Frog: Mindfulness Exercises for Kids*, Pap/Com edition (Boston: Shambhala Publications Inc, 2014)

GENERAL PARENTING/LIFESTYLE BOOKS

Bryson, Dr Tina Payne, and Siegel, Dr Daniel, *The Whole-Brain Child: 12 Proven Strategies to Nurture Your Child's Developing Mind*, 1st edition (London: Robinson, 2012)

Chandra, Sheila, *Banish Clutter Forever: How the Toothbrush Principle Will Change Your Life* (London: Vermilion, 2010)

Cohen, Lawrence J., *Playful Parenting*, Reprint edition (New York: Ballantine Books, 2012)

Faber, Adele, and Mazlish, Elaine, *How To Talk So Kids Will Listen and Listen So Kids Will Talk*, 3rd edition (London: Piccadilly Press, 2013)

González, Carlos, *My Child Won't Eat!: How to Enjoy Mealtimes without Worry*, 2, Revised and updated edition (London: Pinter & Martin Ltd, 2012)

Hatch, Amber, *Nappy Free Baby: a Practical Guide to Baby-led Potty Training from Birth* (London: Vermilion, 2015)

Jackson, Deborah, *Letting Go as Children Grow: From Early Intimacy to Full Independence – a Parent's Guide*, New edition (London: Bloomsbury Publishing PLC, 2003)

Payne, Kim John, *Simplicity Parenting: Using the Extraordinary Power of Less to Raise Calmer, Happier, and More Secure Kids* (New York: Ballantine Books Inc., 2010)

Rapley, Gill, and Murkett, Tracey, *Baby-Led Weaning: Helping Your Baby to Love Good Food* (London: Vermilion, 2008)

GENERAL MINDFULNESS AND MEDITATION BOOKS

Bhikkhu, Ajahn Buddhadasa, *Mindfulness with Breathing: A Manual for Serious Beginners*, trans. by Bhikkhu Santikaro, Revised edition (Boston: Wisdom Publications,U. S., 1998)

Goldstein, Joseph, and Kornfield, Jack, *Seeking the Heart of Wisdom: The Path of Insight Meditation*, Reprint edition (Boston: Shambhala Publications Inc, 2001)

Thich Nhat Hanh, *The Miracle of Mindfulness: A Manual on Meditation* (London: Rider, 1991)

———, *Peace Is Every Step: The Path of Mindfulness in Everyday Life*, 1st edition (London: Rider, 1991)

Levine, Stephen, *A Gradual Awakening* (Garden City, N. Y.: Anchor Books/ Doubleday, 1979)

Paramananda, *Change Your Mind: Practical Guide to Buddhist Meditation*, New edition (Birmingham, Eng.: Windhorse Publications, 2005)

Salzberg, Sharon, *Lovingkindness: The Revolutionary Art of Happiness*, Revised edition (Boston: Shambhala Publications Inc, 2002)

Silverton, Sarah, and Kabat-Zinn, Jon, *Mindfulness Breakthrough: The Revolutionary Approach to Dealing with Stress, Anxiety and Depression* (London: Watkins Publishing Ltd, 2012)

Sweet, Corinne, and Mihotich, Marcia, *The Mindfulness Journal: Exercises to Help You Find Peace and Calm Wherever You Are*, Main Market edition (Boxtree, 2014)

Williams, Mark, Teasdale, John, Segal, Zindel, and Kabat-Zinn, Jon, *The Mindful Way Through Depression: Freeing Yourself from Chronic Unhappiness*, 1 Pap/Com edition (New York: Guilford Press, 2007)

Williams, Prof Mark, and Penman, Danny, *Mindfulness: A Practical Guide to Finding Peace in a Frantic World* (London: Piatkus, 2011)

Useful Websites

MEDITATION CLASSES AND RETREAT CENTRES

www.dharma.org – Insight Meditation Society retreat centre in
  Massachusetts, USA

www.gaiahouse.co.uk – Retreat centre in Devon, UK

www.holyisland.org – Buddhist retreat centre in Scotland, UK

www.mindfulness-network.org – UK listing of accredited mindfulness
  teachers and good practice guidelines

www.mindfulnessbell.org – International sanghas (communities) associated
  with Thich Nhat Hanh

www.newforestmindfulness.com – UK centre offering mindfulness and
  psychotherapy, including Mindfulness for Childbirth and Parenting

www.plumvillage.org – Retreat centre in France, home of Thich Nhat Hanh,
  plus other retreat centres worldwide.

www.samatha.org – A lay Buddhist organization in the UK, Ireland and
  USA, offering classes and retreats at its centre in Wales

www.thebuddhistcentre.com – Triratna is an international Buddhist
  organization offering classes and retreats

WEBSITES OFFERING AUDIO MEDITATIONS

www.diydharma.org – A collection of various teachers offering talks and
  meditations

www.franticworld.com/free-meditations-from-mindfulness – Guided
  meditations from the 8-week MBCT course devised at the Oxford Mindfulness Centre

www.freebuddhistaudio.com/meditation/ – Talks and meditations
www.tnhaudio.org – Talks and meditations by Thich Nhat Hanh and others

WEBSITES ON COMMUNITY-SHARING RESOURCES

www.freecycle.org – International networking site to give and receive items
www.liftshare.com – UK networking site for sharing journeys
www.streetbank.com – UK site connecting neighbours with each other for
   sharing skills and resources.
www.volunteermatch.org – International site for volunteering opportunities

WATKINS

Sharing Wisdom Since
1893

The story of Watkins dates back to 1893, when the scholar of esotericism John Watkins founded a bookshop, inspired by the lament of his friend and teacher Madame Blavatsky that there was nowhere in London to buy books on mysticism, occultism or metaphysics. That moment marked the birth of Watkins, soon to become the home of many of the leading lights of spiritual literature, including Carl Jung, Rudolf Steiner, Alice Bailey and Chögyam Trungpa.

Today, the passion at Watkins Publishing for vigorous questioning is still resolute. Our wide-ranging and stimulating list reflects the development of spiritual thinking and new science over the past 120 years. We remain at the cutting edge, committed to publishing books that change lives.

DISCOVER MORE . . .

Read our blog

Watch and listen to
our authors in action

Sign up to
our mailing list

JOIN IN THE CONVERSATION

 WatkinsPublishing   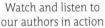 @watkinswisdom

 watkinsbooks    watkinswisdom    watkins-media

Our books celebrate conscious, passionate, wise and happy living.
Be part of the community by visiting

www.watkinspublishing.com